LIFE WITH MOTHER TERESA

Life with Mother Teresa

My Thirty-Year Friendship
with the
Mother of the Poor

FR. SEBASTIAN VAZHAKALA, M.C.

SERVANT BOOKS

PUBLISHED BY ST. ANTHONY MESSENGER PRESS
CINCINNATI, OHIO

Life with Mother Teresa was published originally as *Vita con Madre Teresa: Testimonianze, lettere, immagini inedite*, copyright ©2003, by Elvetica Edizioni S.A., Switzerland.

Library of Congress Cataloging-in-Publication Data

Vazhakala, Sebastian.
[Vita con Madre Teresa. English]
Life with Mother Teresa : my thirty-year friendship with the Mother of the Poor / by Sebastian Vazhakala.
p. cm.
Includes index.
ISBN 0-86716-622-3 (alk. paper)
1. Teresa, Mother, 1910– 2. Missionaries of Charity. 3. Vazhakala, Sebastian. I. Title.

BX4406.5.Z8V3913 2004
271'.97—dc22

2004020302

Cover design by Candle Light Studio
Book design by Sandy L. Digman

ISBN 0-87616-622-3

Published by Servant Books, an imprint of
St. Anthony Messenger Press

Printed in the United States of America

Contents

Introduction

This book comes from my personal knowledge of our beloved and Blessed Mother Teresa of Calcutta, from March 1966 through July 1997.

The first time I heard Mother Teresa speak was at St. Albert's College in Ranchi, India. I was doing my studies in philosophy at the college, and she came to address the staff and the students in March 1966. I met her personally at noon on November 30, 1966, in the motherhouse parlor in Calcutta. (In January 2001 the Indian government officially changed the city's name to Kolkata. We have used the name Calcutta throughout this book, as it is familiar to many.)

The last time I was with Mother Teresa was on July 19, 1997. I was the main celebrant at a Mass at the sisters' house at 222 Via Casilina in Rome. After the Holy Mass she started talking to us brothers in the chapel. A sister came to wheel her away in her wheelchair, and Mother told us to go have breakfast. While we were doing so, she sent the regional superior, Sr. Elena, to ask us to stay afterward so that she could talk with us again in the chapel. She came in her wheelchair and spoke to us for over forty-five minutes about humility and charity and how to become holy. The only way to humility, she told us, is to accept joyfully all the humiliations, mistreatments, and trials of everyday life.

One of the brothers asked, "Mother, who is your favorite saint?"

She said without waiting for him to finish the question, "Our Lady."

The brother was not happy with the answer. "But Our Lady is very special. Who else?"

She said, "St. Joseph"—in other words, the Holy Family.

She told us to keep praying for China. She told us not to get preoccupied with many useless things but to concentrate on Jesus and His life and mission. She blessed us all.

She did not want to stop. She repeated some things many times, as she tended to forget what she had said a minute before. She had totally surrendered her memory, her will, everything. These things the Lord had taken away from her, but remaining with her were His grace and His love. This was enough for Our Lord, for her and for us.

On the afternoon of that same day, Br. Charbel and I accompanied her to the airport along with some sisters and others. We were given the VIP room, where she enquired about how things were with the brothers. She wrote a few notes for us and for the Lay Missionaries of Charity, and then she had me sit closer to her.

She spoke with me about the Corpus Christi Movement, an international movement she had founded, with the blessing of Pope John Paul II, for diocesan priests. Fr. Pasquale Cervara, the coordinator of Corpus Christi, was present. Her last words to me were "I want you to be a part of it."

By then the Air India official had come to take her to the aircraft. Our eyes were full, as we all felt that perhaps it was the last time we would see her in this world. It was a symbolic take-off. Air India would not bring her to the home of her heavenly Father, but her hour would soon come.

Mother Teresa's last letter to me is dated August 23, 1997. It was a short note of recommendation for an elderly person who wanted to become a priest.

I talked to her on the telephone from our house in Albania on August 26, 1997, her eighty-seventh birthday. She sounded quite well. "How are you, Fr. Sebastian, and how are all the brothers? You are always in my prayers. Pray much for Mother. All right."

I told her that twenty-six of us were on our annual retreat, to which she replied, "Thank God for the vocations and try to help them to become holy. Pray much for Mother. God bless you.... If you need anything, do not hesitate to ask the sisters.

God bless you. Mother loves you." This was the last time that I spoke with Mother.

Her hour arrived on September 5, the first Friday of the month. That is when her immortal soul flew from her frail, old, worn-out body to be with the Source of life and love for all eternity. She would be like a piece of iron stuck to its magnet once and for all, destined to carry on her mission of loving service from the throne of the Most High God.

Thirty-one years of knowing a person. In one sense I knew her more than my own mother, whom I loved so much. With my mother I lived nineteen years, most of which I spent at school. But with Mother Teresa I spent the best part of my life, working with the poor in various parts of the world. She used to say, "We know each other by heart."

What I am going to narrate in the following pages, then, is primarily from my own personal knowledge of Mother Teresa, stemming from opportunities I had to be with her in various parts of the world, sometimes visiting persons of importance. There are also her letters to me. I have so far found eighty-one of these, most of which are handwritten.

The last but not least source of my knowledge about Mother Teresa was Lazar Bojaxhiu, her dearly beloved brother, who became my friend and spiritual child. I had the good fortune to lead Lazar through his final days in the summer of 1981. I'll begin with what I learned from Lazar, because it relates to a large extent to Mother's childhood.

PART I

Remembering Mother Teresa

CHAPTER ONE

LAZAR REMEMBERS

I met Lazar for the first time at Via di San Agapito in Rome, in December 1979, shortly after Mother received the Nobel Prize. Fortunately I have a picture of the two of them together at our place. Starting with that first meeting, Lazar and I became close friends, and I had several long and interesting conversations with him.

Lazar was two years older than Mother Teresa. He was born on August 24, 1908, and Mother was born August 26, 1910, in Skopje, Macedonia. They had one older sister, Aga. Lazar told me that their mother had Mother Teresa baptized the day after she was born, because two previous children had died soon after birth. They named her Agnes Gonxha Bojaxhiu and called her Gonxha, which means "flower bud." She would eventually become the "Little Flower," as she took the name Teresa at her first profession.

The First School of Charity

Lazar said that as a girl Mother Teresa was very pretty, happy, and energetic. She was their mother's pet. She sang as a soloist, and her father sang in the choir.

Trials and suffering were part of Mother's life from an early age. One night her father, who was an active campaigner for the reunion of Albania, went out for a meeting. He came back quite late and started vomiting. The family rushed him to the hospital, but it was no use. He went home to God.

It was 1919, and Gonxha was only nine years old. Their father had been a partner in an Italian company. The sudden death of this beloved man brought not only great sadness but also miserable poverty.

Gonxha missed her father very much, though her mother tried her best to fulfill both parental roles. Lazar said that Drana was a woman of extraordinary faith with great organizing abilities. What Mother Teresa became, what she represents today, is due to her mother. In fact, Lazar called Mother Teresa an exact copy of their mother. If he could, he said, he would build a monument in honor of Drana.

Drana's sweet home was the first school of charity for Mother Teresa. Her beloved mother's words and example stayed with her even until she died. For example, she would often recall her mother's lesson of how one bad person can corrupt others: "One day," Mother said, "my mother brought a basket full of good apples. The following day she put a rotten apple on the top of the good ones. Within a few days the apples that were in contact with the rotten one were all affected."

Drana visited poor people, sometimes bringing them to the family's home to take care of them and share with them all the comforts she could. In a letter of 1937, Drana reminded Mother Teresa of one of those people:

> Dear child, do not forget that you went out to India for the sake of the poor. Do you remember "Filé"? She was covered in sores, but what made her suffer much more was the knowledge that she was alone in the world. We did what we could for her. But the worst thing was not the sores, it was the fact that she had been forgotten by her family.

In the Bojaxhu home, family prayer was obligatory, at meals and other daily times. Later Mother Teresa liked to quote the old saying, "The family that prays together stays together."

"You see, Fr. Sebastian," Lazar said, "Mother Teresa did not fall from the sky. She had her training at home. Today you may say—and she too may think—that God did all that. God prepared her."

From this we can see how important family training is for children. Mother Teresa repeatedly said, "Let your community, your family, be another Nazareth."

Gonxha was a good student, Lazar said, a very good example to everybody, and a leader of the choir both in school and at church. Her love for Our Lady was apparent at an early age, as she joined the Marian Sodality. She was very outgoing, and people were attracted spontaneously to her. She had a tender and respectful love for Jesus. This would become a spousal love when she consecrated herself totally to God through the vows of chastity, poverty, and obedience.

Lazar left his mother and two sisters in 1924 to pursue higher studies in Austria, as he had received a scholarship. Later he settled in Tirana, the capital of Albania, and continued his training at a military academy. His older sister came to live with him in Tirana, leaving their mother alone in Skopje. These two worked to convince Drana to move to Tirana, and in 1934 she finally did so.

In July 1972, Drana was ninety-three years old and dying. Mother Teresa tried every possible way to go see her, but it was impossible. Later she wrote me:

> My mother had not seen me for forty-six years. Months before she died, she kept calling, and longing to see me, her youngest child. Albania being what it is, no Indian is allowed to go. I could go so near, and yet not to her. So she died with my name in her mouth.

Mother Teresa wanted to get her sister out of Albania, but she did not have the joy of seeing her again in this world. Aga went home to God a year after her mother's death.

Lazar and God

Lazar came to Italy as a political refugee in 1949. He married a woman named Maria, from Florence, and they settled in Palermo, Sicily. They had one daughter, Agé.

Although Lazar believed in God, loved his family, and took care of them to the best of his ability, he was not a practicing Catholic. The discovery that he had cancer precipitated a serious crisis in his life. Mother Teresa spent hours trying to convince him of the importance of making his confession and of reviving his sacramental life.

They spoke in Croatian. Lazar did not know English, but he knew French, German, and Albanian. Mother had forgotten her Albanian, and she did not speak French or German. Both knew Croatian very well, as they had had their schooling in that language.

By the way, Mother said that when she first heard people speaking English, she thought they had stones in their mouths. It took a long time for her to learn the language. She used to say, "My English, my English!"

Lazar finally consented to make his confession, provided Mother Teresa call and ask me to hear it. He said he did not trust many priests, but he would make his confession to me. Mother telephoned and told me to come to St. John Lateran, which is the vicariate of Rome, where they were both going to be that morning. After their appointment I was invited to accompany them to the sisters' house at San Gregorio al Celio. This I did, and Lazar made his confession there.

Afterward Lazar said, "I have a question: Why should I suffer so much? I have not done anything seriously wrong."

I smiled and said, "You know that the whole world and you yourself think that your sister is a great saint. When she dies and goes home to God, she will have a wonderful place close to Jesus, and you her brother will be so far from her. Then you won't be able to do anything. But now, if you offer your suffering in union with the suffering of Jesus, you too can be closer to Him and to your sister in the world to come." Of course, this wasn't such a convincing answer. But he accepted it and went on.

I visited him practically every day in Villa Flaminia, a private nursing home in Rome, where he stayed for about three weeks. The doctors ran all the tests and analyses they could think of running, but they couldn't do much for him. So Mother brought him to San Gregorio al Celio, where I also visited him.

Finally Lazar returned to Palermo, where Mother Teresa visited him in May 1981, about a month and a half before he left this world for God. During my first visit there, I celebrated Holy Mass at his home. On a second occasion I also anointed him, as his condition was becoming increasingly critical. I tried to visit a third time, but before I reached Palermo he died. I celebrated the funeral the following day. Mother Teresa was visiting the sisters in Venezuela.

Lazar was a good man, loving and caring. He loved the Missionary of Charity Sisters in Palermo as if they were his own daughters. He used to telephone the sisters at Tor Fiscale in Rome and ask them to sing a song that begins, "Quel mattino andavamo per due strade, voglio la felicità." It means, "That morning we were going in two directions; I want happiness."

Lazar's wife lived a few more years. Both she and Agé kept in contact with us and remained part of our "family." Agé once organized a meeting in Palermo at which I was the main speaker. At that time I celebrated Holy Mass in the sisters' church, and many people attended.

CHAPTER TWO

MOTHER'S OTHER BROTHERS

The apostles' eyes were opened with the resurrection apparitions. The Gospel of Luke tells us that Jesus was "made known to them in the breaking of the bread," and "He opened their minds to understand the Scriptures" (Lk 24:35, 45). The experience of Pentecost gave them what we could call a "transfigured memory"—that is, they began to see everything in the light of the Paschal mystery, with clarity and conviction.

Something similar happens to us who try to bring home all the various experiences we have had with Mother Teresa over the years. In lingering over these memories, I renew in my own heart a deep love for God and commitment to His call. And as the four evangelists documented Jesus' life for the sake of believers yet to come, I write of Mother Teresa so that you might know this saint and follow her example of love.

A New Congregation

I still remember that first meeting in the motherhouse parlor in Calcutta in March 1966. Mother wasn't a world-renowned personality then. I was still a philosophy student at St. Albert's College, and I was in Calcutta for a week to see how the newly born Pious Union of Brothers lived. I expressed to Mother Teresa my desire to join the brothers and to continue my studies for the priesthood. She was more than happy about this. She explained to me in simple terms what the brothers do and what their life-style is like:

> It is God's work we do. It is not social work or humanitarian service: Whatever we do to anyone we do to Jesus, and we are called to serve the poorest of the poor people. We also try to live a simple and poor life. Many of the comforts you may have been used to have, you may not find them anymore and you must be ready to make many sacrifices.

I told her that was why I wanted to join the brothers.

A few months later I saw Mother Teresa again, on Easter Sunday afternoon, March 26, 1967. She came with the Archbishop of Calcutta, Msgr. Albert D'Souza, for the canonical elevation of the Pious Union of the Missionary Brothers of Charity of Calcutta into a diocesan religious congregation. It was "God's Easter gift to Calcutta's poor," the *Catholic Herald of Calcutta* announced. Mother was overjoyed, and she shared her joy with all of us.

I had come from St. Albert's to spend Holy Week. The climax of the week for me was my formal entry into the Pious Union of Brothers on Holy Thursday night. The brothers had already moved to their motherhouse at 7 Mansatala Row. There were thirteen brothers at the time, counting myself.

Mother told us how she had obtained ecclesiastical recognition for the brothers—from Propaganda Fide in Rome—and also of the great responsibilities we now had. We had light refreshments afterward, then Mother and the archbishop and others prepared to leave. Mother's presence always brought much joy and great peace. As she was leaving she kept saying, "Let us thank God for this great gift, let us thank God for this new congregation, and let your life be your first form of thanksgiving. Pray for Mother. Mother prays much for all of you."

The next afternoon we participated in the blessing of the Dhappa Leprosy Centre. Mother Teresa was there, along with some sisters, brothers, and important Calcutta officials. The Gospel passage chosen for the occasion was Luke 17:11-19, Jesus healing the ten lepers.

Mother spoke to us with conviction: We should not make the leprosy patients feel rejected and unwanted; we must love them as Jesus loves them and serve them as He serves them. The more repugnant a person is, she said, the more faith we need in order to see Jesus in the person: the way we look at, the way we wash, the way we hold him or her—with tenderness, with love and compassion.

This was the first time in my life I had seen leprosy patients. To be honest, I was frightened. On my way back to Ranchi, I wondered whether I would ever be able to serve these people. Would I have the courage to face them? I needed confirmation of the decision I had made to leave the diocese and join the Missionaries of Charity.

Once back in Ranchi, I finished my final exams. Then I returned as quickly as possible—on April 7, 1967, to be exact—to Calcutta to work with the poorest of the poor.

Formation Year

Twelve of us began our historical novitiate under Br. Andrew on June 2, 1967, the Feast of the Sacred Heart. After Holy Mass we knelt and prayed, and then Br. Andrew blessed us and offered us to the Most Sacred Heart of Jesus. Mother Teresa wasn't present but sent us all prayerful greetings—welcoming, encouraging words.

For me it was like a dream being slowly realized. After my five years of study in languages, philosophy, and teaching, here I was starting the first lessons of prayers and starting this new way of life as a Missionary of Charity. All of us were beginners; there was no senior group to which we could look for examples and guidance. But there was the Holy Family of Nazareth, in which Jesus prepared Himself for His impending mission of love.

Mother Teresa had begun the Pious Union of Brothers on March 25, 1963, the Feast of the Annunciation. Two of the original brothers could not face the hardships of the life of the Missionaries of Charity, so they eventually left the little group. Br. Andrew, a Jesuit from Melbourne, Australia, stayed on, as did Br. Joseph Michael of Calcutta, who was my inspiration in the Missionary of Charity way of doing things. Br. Aloysius from Madhya Pradesh was the next longest surviving member; his two sisters were also Missionaries of Charity. Then came Br. Damien from Kerala, Br. Ignatius from Madhya Pradesh, Br. Benedict from Sri Lanka, Br. George and Br. James from Kerala, Br. Bernard from Bihar, Br. John from Kerala, Br. David from West Bengal, Br. Iswardas from Utter Pradesh, and myself from Kerala.

There were many special moments of grace during my year of formation. One of the first was when the pilgrim statue of Our Lady of Fatima arrived in Calcutta. I saw

Mother's devotion to Mary that day. Her face lit up; she was like a little girl seeing her beloved mother after a lapse of some weeks or months.

Another occasion was Christmas Day, when we had the children's Christmas party. It was a gathering of all the street and slum children we were taking care of, over five thousand of them from various parts of the crowded and chaotic city of Calcutta. Mother Teresa and the sisters joyfully shared with all the children the beautiful Christmas gifts they had prepared, including some sports equipment. They organized races and other games for the children.

This was my first Christmas outside Catholic circles. It opened my eyes to a wider horizon. I was deeply aware of the fact that Jesus was born not only for a few Christians but for all mankind, irrespective of caste, color, or religion.

There was so much to learn—so much that my five years of seminary formation had not given me. I knew how to prove the existence of God by use of reason, but here I was seeing His love and care for all people, especially for the poorest of the poor. Philosophy taught me that every person possesses an immortal soul, but never had I thought that every person I touched, every person I served, was Jesus. It was on that Christmas Day—which for me was my first real Christmas, even though I was twenty-five years old—that the horizons of my life opened. My joy was beyond description.

All the more I began to appreciate my novitiate, the purpose of which was to help me live less and less for myself and more and more for God and for others. The words of St. John the Baptist began to make more sense in my life: "[Jesus] must increase, but I must decrease" (Jn 3: 30). My novitiate became a real school of living a true Christian life.

In January 1968 it happened that Br. Benedict and I fell ill with chicken pox. We were isolated from the rest of the community, up on the terrace under the water tanks, where there were two beds. My condition became quite serious.

Quite late one night, as I felt worse, Br. Andrew called the sisters' motherhouse. Mother Teresa came with Sr. (and Dr.) Gertrude right away. It was then that I experienced a mother's love in a way that I had not since I left my own sweet home. Mother was tender, concerned, loving, and caring. She and Sr. Gertrude cleaned and arranged the room, then made sure we were quite comfortable.

They repeated this care a couple times until we recovered. Mother always would say with a smile when I thanked her, "All for Jesus, Brother. You too offer all to Jesus."

"Yes, Mother, whatever you do, your tender love and concern is all for Jesus."

As my novitiate continued, I felt deeply the warmth of a mother. I sometimes questioned whether I deserved all this tender care!

First Vows

After I was better, the brothers had me accompany an ill person to Mother's Home for the Dying in Kalighat, a district of Calcutta. Mother was taking care of another patient when we arrived. When she finished, she made the usual enquiries about the brothers, their life, and their work.

And then, out of the clear blue sky, she asked me whether I knew that six of the brothers were going to make their first vows after the canonical year. This was a matter of necessity, as there were no senior brothers to manage our second house in Dumdum. Mother Teresa suggested I speak with Br. Andrew about taking my vows also. I spoke with him at an opportune time, and I was added to the number, even though I was "untimely born" as the last one in the senior group. All the others—Br. Andrew, Br. Joseph Michael, Br. Aloysius, Br. Damien, Br. George, and Br. Benedict—had been with the pious union two years or more.

In preparation for our vows, we had a wonderful eight days of the Ignatian Spiritual Exercises, preached by a Belgian Jesuit, Fr. Mather Shillings. The night before our profession we all wrote out our vow formula. On the morning of June 2, Msgr. Eric Barber, the vicar general of Calcutta, was the main celebrant at a Holy Mass on the terrace of the brothers' house at 7 Mansatala Row. Mother Teresa, Sr. Agnes, and some of the senior sisters were present at this historic event: the first brothers' profession Mass.

To my great surprise Br. Joseph Michael, the very first of the brothers to join, backed out from our line. It shocked me deeply, as he was the person to whom I looked as my example, someone from whom I could always learn something new. So just six of us made vows on that historic Pentecost Sunday, June 2, 1968. God's ways are mysterious.

The day after our profession we all scattered, like the Apostles after Pentecost. Br. George was appointed local servant of the community in Dumdum, where for almost ten months Br. Felix, then just a candidate, had been serving; Br. Aloysius and Br. Damien remained at our Mansatala house; Br. Benedict was assigned to Watgung to work with some orphan boys; Br. Andrew would continue his work with the other novices; and I went to the Papal Athenaeum in Pune to finish my studies for the priesthood. There I would be for four years.

During this period Mother made trips to Pune, mainly to visit the sisters there. It happened that one of our professors wasn't too happy about Mother Teresa's opening houses outside India, especially in Europe, plus going to the West wearing an Indian sari. So I arranged for him to meet Mother.

They talked for over an hour, after which I asked the professor, "Father, how did the talk go?" He replied to the effect that, as Mother was so convinced and clear about what she was doing, who would be able to persuade her to the contrary? But Mother told me later that they had had a very lively discussion and exchange of ideas.

"Something Beautiful for God"

In April 1969 noted British correspondent Malcolm Muggeridge came to Calcutta to videotape Mother Teresa's Missionaries of Charity for B.B.C. London. She did not want him to focus on her but rather on the work she was doing and the kind of people she was serving. She told him, "Together let us do something beautiful for God."

This was the first film about Mother, and a book followed by the same author and under the same title, the one Mother had suggested: *Something Beautiful for God*. The life and work of Mother Teresa, till then known mainly in the East, was now going to be put "on the lampstand," where this holy woman's light would "shine before others, so that they may see your good works and give glory to your Father in heaven" (see Mt 5:14-16).

So it happened that one fine morning in April 1969, Br. Andrew told me to accompany him on his motorbike to our house in Dumdum, which is near the International Airport in Calcutta. He told me that the television people might want to interview me. So we assembled with Mother Teresa on the balcony of the brothers' house, to receive the whole crew of Mr. Malcolm Muggeridge.

While Mr. Muggeridge interviewed Br. Andrew, Mother

Teresa and I sat and talked about the brothers and various things. Then Mr. Muggeridge wanted the brothers to go downstairs and form a line with our orphan boys. The camera focused on the boys, while the rosary beads kept moving through Mother's fingers in the room upstairs. When all was done, Mr. Muggeridge told her, "Excellent, Mother. It came out very well."

"Thank God. Let us thank Our Lady," she said.

The film crew was ready to move on to other sites. Within minutes the jeep was ready. Br. Andrew told me to go with Mother and Mr. Muggeridge; he would stay at the house. I cheerfully obliged.

As we passed the Loreto convent, Mother Teresa recalled her nineteen years there. "It was a very wonderful time," she said. "I can't forget all that Loreto did for me and how through Loreto the good Lord prepared me for this life."

In fact, Mother always used whatever she found helpful and, in accordance with the Spirit and her charism, without any scruples. She had her way of speaking and of doing things, which opened people up to God and to the Missionaries of Charity. She never pretended that everyone could live the way she lived. But she happily welcomed those who showed any interest in her work. She respected all and despised no one, while holding to what she believed to be good and true for herself and for the Missionaries of Charity.

CHAPTER THREE

A GOOD MOTHER TO ME

My studies advanced, and I enjoyed them thoroughly. As my day of ordination to the priesthood approached, I wrote Mother Teresa to tell her the date, place, and time, inviting her to be present for this uniquely graced occasion. Her reply was prompt, dated September 22, 1971:

> My dear Brother Sebastian,
>
> Thanks for your letter. It is painful for me not to be present at your first sacrifice, but you know through this my sacrifice I will be closer to you. My prayers will be with you. I am leaving tomorrow for England, Rome, and then on the thirteenth I will take five Sisters to New York for the new foundation.
>
> You must keep this house very close to your heart, as it is being founded together with your ordination. Keep the joy of Christ always as your strength. God bless you.
> Mother

Although her reply was negative, I still felt happy. On the back of one of her photographs she had written:

A PRIEST—today, tomorrow, for ever.
HIS CHOSEN ONE.
The ONLY ONE who brings CHRIST on the altar.
The ONLY ONE who can say: "This is my body,
this is my blood,"
and you, my brother, are HIS PRIEST.
God bless you.
Mother

We celebrated the profession of some of our brothers the morning of June 2, 1972, at St. Ignatius Church in the Ekbalpore district of Calcutta. Mother and some sisters were present. After Holy Mass she almost ran to me, took my hands, and congratulated me. At first I did not understand why she was doing this, but then I realized that it was our first meeting after my ordination. She remembered—like a good mother.

Mother's Care

Mother's loving concern and her delicate charity and thoughtfulness were ever abiding, even in the midst of confusion and chaos. Her smile was always uplifting and strengthening. She was a person who did ordinary things with extraordinary love and devotion. She spoke so often about how thoughtful we should be, which was confirmed by her words and actions.

One Sunday in September 1972, I was celebrating the Holy Sacrifice of the Mass in the Home for the Dying. I had a very high fever and a cough as well. It was my third Mass of the morning.

As I finished the Mass, Mother Teresa came over to me and said, "Fr. Sebastian, I want you to come with me to the motherhouse."

We passed by our house, and I told the brothers where we were going. As we reached the motherhouse, Mother

Teresa called Sr. Gertrude, who came in and examined me, made me eat and drink something, and gave me some medical treatment. Mother told Sr. Gertrude to take care of me and to get me x-rayed. This was done the following day.

Later Mother called me on the phone to see how I was. She told me that she was going to take me to Green Park, a sisters' house near Calcutta's airport, where I could rest for a week or more. So she herself came in the ambulance and took me straight to the sisters' place, which was above a children's home. She told the sisters to feed me nicely and make me rest.

The sisters were very obedient to Mother Teresa. Every morning I celebrated the Holy Mass with them, and then I read, prayed, ate, and slept.

A few days later Mother came to see how I was, to see that all her orders had been carried out, and to see that I was cooperating with the sisters. Her love and care were constant. She had a way of making me—and others, I'm sure—really feel that life is worth living. She knew that each person is important. She would often say, "We are not just a number.... A sister, a brother, is more than just a number. Each person is wanted and loved by God."

On another occasion I was celebrating Holy Mass in the Home for the Dying. After the Mass Mother said to me, "I want you to go to Shantinagar for me."

It was almost midday. Shantinagar is about 120 miles from Calcutta, perhaps more. The way there wasn't easy. Besides, I had never been there. She told me to go to our sisters in Asensol first and spend the night there. The following morning Sr. Alice, the superior, would take me to Shantinagar.

I said yes to Mother Teresa, but first I had to go to our house and inform the brothers of the errand. On the way I reflected on this plan. I realized that Mother had seen me looking a bit down, and she thought that perhaps a little outing would cheer me up. The closer one is to God, the closer one comes also to human beings, and the better one sees their needs. That is real love, understanding love, and enduring love.

Mother Teresa from the very beginning showed great concern for me and took tender care of me. So much so that the sisters used to tell me that I should not go to see Mother in their convents, because "Mother forgets all of us when she sees you." Whether true or not, I can say that from the time I met her in November 1966 in the motherhouse parlor, we remained very close. She was always a mother to me, and though unworthy, I have always considered myself to be her son!

Graceful Humility

Mother was human too. Once she was speaking to me about distributing Holy Communion in the motherhouse, as there are so many Sisters there. I asked her, "Mother, why don't you help distribute Holy Communion? One person alone takes so much time."

She said, "No, Jesus never did that."

I told her, "Jesus gave the loaves to the Apostles to distribute."

She became upset, and it took time for her to reconcile with me afterward. Some years later not only did she start distributing Holy Communion but so did many of the senior superior sisters. It wasn't the right time when I suggested it. There is a time for everything, as Ecclesiastes 3:1-8 points out.

On the eve of India's Independence Day Mother telephoned me. From the tone of her voice it was clear that something was not quite right.

"Yes, Mother, what happened?"

She said, "I don't want you to celebrate any Hindu Mass in Kalighat tomorrow."

Then only I remembered I had told the sister in charge that we would celebrate the Holy Mass as we used to do in our house at 7 Mansatala Row. I tried to explain to Mother Teresa that it wasn't a Hindu Mass but a Mass incorporating a few traditional elements of Hindu culture. We would have three people process forward, one carrying a candle, another incense, and a third flowers. But Mother wouldn't hear of it. So I agreed to her wishes, and we had the usual celebration.

Once one of the Missionary of Charity priest brothers refused to wear the chasuble for a Mass in one of the convents, using only an alb and a stole. The sister superior reported the matter to Mother Teresa. She called for the brother, who stood his ground. He was even ready not to celebrate Mass rather than change his decision.

Mother told me, "Br. Sebastian, can you imagine that Br. So-and-So refused to wear the chasuble? I didn't want the sisters to go without daily Mass, and so I told him to continue celebrating the Holy Mass with alb and stole only." She found it hard to accept such refusals, especially from one of her own brothers. Still she said, "It is all right, all for Jesus." We are just pencils in the hands of God.

Beginning June 2, 1972, I was in charge of the novices—fifty of them. Mother told me to teach them the true spirit of our society. I invited her occasionally to come to speak to our novices. In fact, whenever she was in the motherhouse and was more or less free, I would bring her to our novitiate.

It was best, she said, to come with the ambulance and get her. Once we were riding in the ambulance, and she spoke of her health. She was not feeling too well, she said. She was sure that it was because she had accepted food from someone.

"This was the result of my own disobedience," she said. "It taught me a lesson: that I should not eat anything outside of our convent." Of course, she always would take something offered at the brothers' house.

The Brothers' First General Chapter

The little Congregation of the Missionaries of Charity was slowly growing roots and taking shape under the guidance of Mother Teresa and above all Br. Andrew. Many came and saw the newly founded men's order living a simple and poor life, dedicating themselves wholeheartedly and freely to the service of the poorest of the poor. Some stayed on; others tried for a while and then left for one reason or another; and still others left within days or weeks. Ours is a hard and demanding life. Little wonder then that some men leave our institutes for one reason or another, perhaps simply feeling a different kind of call.

We invited Mother to address us on the eve of the first general chapter of the brothers of Calcutta. She came with Sr. Agnes at about eight o'clock in the evening. She talked to us about the purpose for which she had founded the brothers' congregation and how important it was to remain faithful to our spirit and charism, especially poverty:

> We are not a Congregation started to do great and important things but to do ordinary things with extraordinary love, simple things with great love. It is not success that is important but our faithfulness. We are not called to serve the poor people, but to serve the poorest of the poor for whom nobody cares, those whom nobody wants or loves. Remain faithful, Brothers; I beg you all to remain faithful.

It is not that we will not make mistakes. I myself have made thousands of mistakes, but not one of them was made for my own advantage. Jesus did not work any miracles so that he may be known but that people might believe and be saved. Brothers, be kind and compassionate. It is better to make mistakes in kindness than to work miracles in unkindness.

One day a well-dressed man from Europe came to our Home for the Dying. He walked around and saw what we were doing. And as he was going he told me: "Mother Teresa, I wouldn't do this work even for thousands of dollars." I told him that I wouldn't do it either if it were not done for love of Jesus. "What is there that we cannot do today for the love of Jesus!"

Brothers, we are not numbers. We are called to belong to Jesus; we are called to become saints. I remember one of you coming and telling me one time, "Mother Teresa, my vocation is to serve the leprosy patients." I said, "No, Brother. Your vocation is to belong to Jesus."

We must cling to Jesus, like the married couples who leave everything and everybody in order to cling to each other. We are spouses of Christ. Of course, for us women it is easier to understand when we say we are spouses of the Crucified Christ. Be only all for Jesus; be holy.

Mother will pray for you. Pray much for Mother, so that we may not spoil God's work. In this case it is better that our society dies before I die. Our society is founded that God may be praised and glorified. God bless you, Brothers.

The Missionary of Charity Vocation

In 1975 Mother gave a very important talk to the novices:

Let us thank Our Lady for calling us all. Brothers, there were many wonderful sisters in Loreto. Why did He call me? He couldn't find a more miserable one. If He had found one more miserable than I am, He would have

> definitely chosen her. I am sure that He will not find another one more miserable than me.
>
> Why did He call you and not somebody else? It is a mystery.
>
> Every day after Holy Communion I do two things: First of all, I thank God for my vocation, and then I ask for the grace of perseverance. You must do the same. It is not enough to put a habit on, a blue par sari [the official dress of professed sisters], you will be OK. Of course you do not have a habit, except the crucifix. But wear it nicely, Brothers.
>
> I often travel by train from Calcutta to Delhi. And on the way there are two train stations: One is called "Eck dil," which means "one heart." And the other is called "Prempur," "full of love." I often tell the sisters to put the names of the two train stations together and you will have a perfect community: "One heart full of love" in the heart of Jesus and Mary.
>
> Novitiate is an important time. You must know well the Constitutions, to live them, to make your vows according to the Constitutions of the Missionaries of Charity. We do not make our vows according to the Bible or according to some other constitutions. They may be wonderful. We love all religious orders, but we must fall in love with our own.
>
> Let us pray much. Pray for Mother that we may not spoil God's work. God bless you all, Brothers.

On the way back to the motherhouse she asked how the brothers were doing. Did we need anything? Were there any problems? Had any new men expressed interest in the community? Mother would regularly ask these questions of me.

Then she said, "Br. Sebastian, teach them to love Jesus. They seem eager to be holy. I could see in their eyes their eagerness, the way they listened to my talk."

"Yes, Mother. I will try my best to teach them to love Jesus; but you also must come and talk to them."

"Yes, I will, whenever I am in Calcutta. You are my brothers. Now I am leaving for Europe. When I am back, you call me, and I will come."

Mother placed a high priority on supporting us brothers. She would linger on her visits, sometimes canceling appointments in order to spend hours with us.

Jubilee

The Missionary Sisters of Charity celebrated their jubilee year in 1975. The celebration was very edifying. Throughout the year there were prayer services and thanksgiving celebrations in the various religious groups: the Hindus in their temples; the Muslims in their mosques; the followers of Jainism, an ancient way of life rooted in India; and the Buddhists. The dates were fixed in such a way that Mother and some of the senior sisters could be present at each function.

Thanksgiving celebrations were held also in various denominational churches, not only in Calcutta but also in other parts of the country and wherever the Missionary Sisters of Charity had communities. Mother Teresa and the Missionaries of Charity make a fourth vow of wholehearted free service to the poorest of the poor, irrespective of caste, color, creed, or nationality. It was right then for all the religions to give thanks to God in their own way.

The concluding jubilee celebration was in the motherhouse on the anniversary itself, October 7, 1975. This marked the date twenty-five years earlier when the Missionary Sisters of Charity were designated a diocesan congregation. This celebration was mainly for the family of the Missionaries of Charity. At that time there were only the sisters and the brothers—no contemplative branches yet, nor the Missionaries of Charity Fathers, nor the Lay Missionaries of Charity.

It was a very simple celebration. The late Lawrence Cardinal Picachy, who was then archbishop of Calcutta, was the main celebrant of the thanksgiving Mass. Br. Andrew, Br. Damien, Br. Christdas, Br. K.C. Thomas, and I—all Missionary of Charity priests—left our retreat in Dumdum to concelebrate. For me it was wonderful to see the humility, the simplicity, and at the same time Mother's profound gratitude to God. She was so aware that it was God's work she was doing, that it was His and not hers.

We returned to Dumdum after breakfast to resume our retreat. I felt called to a more intense life of prayer, penance, and works of mercy. I also was inspired to get laypeople involved in this ministry, which I thought would take place in God's own time.

CHAPTER FOUR

FIRST AMERICAN MISSIONS

Months later Br. Andrew asked me to go to Los Angeles and open a novitiate. I was not at all eager. But "obedience is better than sacrifice." How could I teach the novices about the sublime value of obedience in the life of a religious if I myself did not obey? So I accepted this request as God's word, made the arrangements, and left for Los Angeles.

I travelled with Br. Andrew to Bangkok, where we stayed for three days. At the airport I knelt down and asked Br. Andrew to bless me, which he did, and I then blessed him. So we said good-bye.

I arrived in Los Angeles June 25, 1976, the Feast of the Sacred Heart that year. On that day Mother Teresa, together with Sr. Nirmala, began their contemplative branch, the Sisters of the Word, at the sisters' house in the Bronx. Mother visited the East Coast a couple of times after that, but never the brothers in Los Angeles. Finally I wrote to say that if she did not visit the brothers in Los Angeles on her next visit, she would not be our Mother anymore. Her reply was loving:

> If I had written all the letters I wrote in my mind, you would have received so many. But my prayer is each day and every day with each one of you, that you may become holy because Jesus, your God, is holy. I am so happy you are all doing well and that you are doing God's work with great love. Today I went to the brothers' and gave them a long talk. Our vocation is to belong to Jesus, and nothing will separate us from the love of Christ. How great is our vocation! How full of joy and holiness we must be out of real gratitude!
>
> I will be in the U.S. by the 17 June [1977], and I hope to be with you at the beginning of July. Then we will tell many things to each other. The sixty-five novices and twenty-three sisters are preparing for first and final vows; so you can imagine the great fervor throughout the house, all preparing for their great day. Keep the joy of Jesus as your strength and the bond of union and peace. God bless you.

Lo and behold, she arrived in Los Angeles as she had written, on July 1, 1977, accompanied by Mrs. Patty Kump, the head of the coworkers in the United States. As we greeted them at the Los Angeles Airport, one of the first things Mother said to me was "I want to be your Mother."

Her words went deep into my heart. I had already forgotten what I had written, but she had not. The passage from Isaiah 49 came to mind: "Can a woman forget her nursing child . . . ? Even these may forget, yet I will not forget you. See, I have inscribed you on the palms of my hands" (Is 49:15-16).

I had never seen Mother so free and joyful, showing a real mother's tender love and care. She prayed with us, cooked and cleaned, ate and sang, taught songs, gave talks, and told us interesting stories.

We had meetings with our coworkers. We had not told them why we were holding Mass that particular afternoon in downtown Los Angeles. Some were dumbfounded when they learned that Mother Teresa was at our house. One of them dropped a parcel and cried aloud in joy and wonder.

Los Angeles has seen many movie stars. Unlike the movie stars, Mother Teresa's presence awakened in the hearts of people the desire for God, for holiness and great peace. Her presence was sacramental and salvific.

Contemplatives in the Heart of the World

At the end of our Eucharistic celebration Mother spoke:

> We'll offer this prayer together, that we may be grateful to God for bringing us together today. And also I'm very grateful to God to have this opportunity to thank you for all the love and care you have shown to our brothers, the love and the trust [with which] you have accepted them and the tender care that you have given to them.
>
> I also want to thank our poor people whom the brothers serve, that they have accepted the brothers with so much love and with so much trust. We owe them very deep gratitude, for if the poor people didn't accept them, I don't think the Missionaries of Charity could exist. And so we are grateful to them for accepting us.
>
> But above all we owe deep gratitude to the Church for allowing us to live, and to be the presence of Jesus among the poorest of the poor and so be God's love and compassion to them. For God still loves the world; He keeps on loving the world. God loved the world so much that He gave His Son, and today He still loves the world and He keeps on giving Jesus through you and through me. Just as Jesus came into the world because God loved the world, His Father loved the world, He was the gift of God for the world. And we too, each one of us in our own way, have to be that love, that compassion of the Father for the world.
>
> And God gave His Son to Mary, the spotless Virgin. And what did she do? The moment she proclaimed that

she was the handmaid of the Lord, that she was empty, that she was nothing, she became full of grace. And we know what she did. With Jesus in her, immediately she wanted to give Jesus to others. But she went there as the handmaid of the Lord, to do the work of a handmaid. And she went in haste, as if she had not enough time to give Him to others. We too! For her it was her First Holy Communion Day, that Jesus came in her life. And so for all of us also. He made Himself Bread of Life that we too, like Mary, become full of Jesus. We too, like her, be in haste to give Him to others. We too, like her, serve others.

And that's why the vocation of the brothers is so beautiful, and the sisters and the coworkers and each one of us: that we have a chance fully to belong to Jesus and that the work that He has entrusted to you and to me and to each one of us is only our love for Him, in a living action. What you do I cannot do, what I do you cannot do, but together we are doing something beautiful for God. That's why Jesus made Himself Bread of Life, to satisfy our hunger for God, our hunger for His love.

But I think that was not enough for Him. He made Himself the hungry one, He made Himself the naked one, He made Himself the homeless one. And He said: I was hungry, I was naked, I was sick, I was homeless, and you did it to me. That's why I say the brothers and sisters are not social workers; they are really contemplatives right in the heart of the world, for they are touching the body of Christ twenty-four hours.

You too in your own homes, in your own life, [to] you too Jesus says the same thing: I was hungry. In your own homes you have the hungry Christ, you have the naked Christ, you have the homeless Christ. In your own home do you recognize Him? Do you know that He is right there? How often the child leaves the home because there is no one to want him. How often the old people are nowhere; they are in an institution because no one has time for them. The poor are right in our own home. Do we know that?

I remember sometime ago a big group of professors from the United States came to our house. And before leaving they said, "Tell us something that will help us, that will help us to become holy."

And I said to them, "Smile at each other." Because we have no time even to look at each other, still less to smile at each other.

And one of them asked me, "Are you married?"

And I said, "Yes, and I find it sometimes very difficult to smile at Jesus, for He can be very demanding."

And I think this is what we have to find: holiness, joy, love in our own homes. We must make our homes another Nazareth where Jesus can come and live with us. For holiness is not the luxury of the few; it is a very simple duty for you and for me. To accept whatever Jesus gives us and to give whatever Jesus takes from us with a big smile is holiness. That's doing God's will.

And so in your life, in my life, in each one of us, God has created us for greater things. He has created us to love and to be loved. And so we come home, and the day comes to go back home, that we may be ready, full of Jesus, to go in haste back home to our Father.

Our poor people are great people. They give us much more than we give to them. We have learned many things from them. They don't need our pity and sympathy, they need our love and compassion. And we must love them not from our abundance, but we must love them until it hurts.

Sometime ago in Calcutta we had no sugar, and I don't know how the word went around that Mother Teresa had no sugar for her children. And a little Hindu child, only four years old, went to his parents, and he told them, "I will not eat sugar for three days. I will give my sugar to Mother Teresa for her children." And the parents had never been to our house before. I didn't know them. They brought the child, and the child gave me the sugar saying, "I have not eaten sugar for three days. Give this to your children." That little one loved with great love because he loved until it hurt.

That evening a man came to our house and told me that a Hindu family with eight children had not eaten for many days. So I took some rice, enough for their dinner, to the family, and I saw the little faces with black dark eyes. Real hunger! The mother took the rice from my hand, and she divided it into two, and she went out.

When she came back I asked her, "What did you do?"

She said, "They are hungry also." The next-door neighbors, a Muslim family, were hungry, and she knew that, and she had the courage and the love to share.

This is something that we have to learn. Just as Jesus allows Himself to be broken, to be given to us as food, we too must break, we must share with each other, with our own people first in our own house for love begins at home. And then with our next-door neighbor, with the people in the street who live with us, and in the town where we are and in the whole world. Love to be true has to hurt. And the people, our people, the poor people, are very great people. Because they give us much love, much joy in accepting us, the little things that we do for them.

Our sisters and brothers are all over the world now, and it is wonderful to see how the people accept us. As they say, "They live the love of Christ for us."

The sisters went to a Muslim country; after eight hundred years a Catholic sister was present in that country. The people were surprised to see young sisters doing what they did. And the governor of that place wrote one of the priests in Rome and said, "The presence of the sisters has lit a new light in the life of our people." And they do not call them Missionaries of Charity; they call them carriers of God's love.

And so you and I, each one of us, have to be that carrier of God's love. Every Holy Communion fills us with Jesus, and we must with Our Lady be in haste to go in

> search and find the child and bring him home. And by bringing him home there is love, there is joy, there is peace, there is God with us.
>
> Pray for us that we may not spoil God's work, that we may continue together with you because the work has been entrusted to you and to us, that together we may do something beautiful for God.

People went home glorifying God. They were so grateful that He had given them such a great and rare gift as Mother Teresa.

A Deeper Poverty

Mother spoke to us about the necessity of being poor like Jesus in an affluent country like America, where the poor are hidden behind huge mansions. Here poverty is deeper and more spiritual in nature.

> There is such a terrible poverty in the West and America, the frightening coldness and indifference of people, so much self-centeredness and pride. Women do not want to be obedient or submissive to their husbands. No wonder there are such terrible problems in families: Children are left alone; older people are dumped into a nursing home.... There are so many alcoholics in Los Angeles, I was told.
>
> Brothers, you are in the midst of such deep poverty and misery. You need to pray much, offer many sacrifices that people begin to love one another and there may be great love, charity, and service. Families do not pray anymore. You know that the family that prays together stays together. Teach the children and the people to pray. Pray with them. Teach them religious songs....
>
> There is much work to do. That is why you have to be holy.... Holiness is not the luxury of the few but the simple duty of you and me. Let us resolve to be holy, for

> God your Lord is holy. Pray much for Mother, that we may not spoil God's work....
>
> As Missionaries of Charity we have the poverty of St. Francis, the obedience of St. Ignatius, and the prayerfulness of St. Benedict. We are called to be contemplative twenty-four hours of the day. Jesus Himself said that "whatever you do to the least of my brethren you do it to Me."

Then Mother taught us several songs, including

> Oh, how I love Jesus,
> oh, how I love Jesus,
> oh, how I love Jesus
> because He first loved me.

There were numerous verses that Mother made up: "For me Jesus is wonderful," "For me Jesus was born like me," "To me Jesus is Bread of Life," and so on, all ending, "Because He first loved me." Mother had a beautiful voice, and she loved to sing about Jesus.

Besides giving us talks, Mother also took time to see all the brothers one by one. My novices were thrilled to be with her. We thanked God again and again for her visit. When we sang together, "Thank you, Father; thank you, Jesus; thank you, Spirit; thank you, Mother," we actually meant Our Lady. But Mother Teresa thought we sang "Mother" for her, so she sang, "Thank you, Jesus," all the louder when we sang, "Thank you, Mother." We laughed a lot about such incidents after her departure.

Faith to Move Mountains

We told Mother about a daytime recreation center in downtown Los Angeles called St. Vincent's Center, run by a priest who was interested in helping the poor. The brothers thought of taking it over. Though His Eminence Cardinal

Timothy Manning was in favor of this, there was a priest who by no means wanted to give it to the brothers.

Mother went with us to the center, a huge building. She said, "Let us make a quick novena to Our Lady," and started nine *Memorares*. When finished she said one more in thanksgiving, and then she put miraculous medals in various parts of the building.

Then we went to the cardinal, to whom Mother said, "We have thrown Our Lady's miraculous medals in St. Vincent's Center."

His Eminence said that that was not enough. "Mother Teresa, you must throw another medal at Father So-and-So's house, too."

Mother asked who the priest was, and on our way to the airport she made us pass by his residence and throw medals. Believe it or not, in two weeks' time the brothers received the news that they could have full charge of St. Vincent's Center! For us it was a miracle.

Mother's faith was simple but firm. She took Jesus' words seriously and literally. She used to say:

> Jesus cannot deceive us. "Whatever you ask in my name, I will give it to you.... Ask and you shall receive, seek and you shall find" [see Jn 16:24; Lk 11:9]. Brothers, do not be afraid to ask: Ask with deep faith; ask with trust. Be like Our Lady—full of love, full of joy, full of charity, full of Jesus. She went in haste to serve her cousin Elizabeth. She was so thoughtful. There was nothing that she couldn't do. She did everything.

Often our problem is that we do not have enough faith. If we have faith, we can move mountains.

During Mother's visit I mentioned to her what I called "the inspiration" I received on October 7, 1975, to lead a deeper life of prayer, penance, and works of mercy. She told me that I was doing well with the brothers, and so I should wait and pray and also talk with Br. Andrew and obey him perfectly.

The devil is powerless over those who humbly, promptly, and joyfully obey the command and even the wishes of the superior. The evil one tried to tempt Jesus several times, from the cradle to the grave. "If you are the Son of God, come down from the cross,... and we will believe" (Mt 27:40, 42). Jesus knew what the devil was up to. He also knew that His mission did not consist in doing spectacular things but in obeying His Father unto death. Jesus is our model.

One of the novices, who was normally very happy and enthusiastic, looked sad and tense in Mother's presence. He always sat at the end of the bench, as far away from her as possible. I asked him the reason for his strange behavior, and he replied that he felt utterly unworthy to be close to such a transparent and saintly person. In her presence he felt like St. Peter facing Jesus after the miraculous catch of fish: "Go away from me, Lord, for I am a sinful man" (Lk 5:8).

All the other brothers were delighted in her presence. Mother Teresa too felt very much at home with her sons. On July 9, she wrote a note of thanks from Guatemala:

> It was a grace for me to be with you all. How great is His love for each one of us. The Sisters were delighted to have your gift in Mexico, and they shared with Guatemala your gift.
>
> Keep praying for me. Everybody this side is well and... doing God's work with great love. For me what joy to be with you and the sisters. Pray for me. God bless you.

CHAPTER FIVE

THE FOUNDING OF THE MISSIONARIES OF CHARITY BROTHERS CONTEMPLATIVE

It can be said that there existed in the seed of Mother's initial call our contemplative branch, which grew up in the silence of faith. It grew from a small group of volunteers in Rome called the Brothers of the Word. Finally, in the fullness of time, God spoke to Mother and to the people who would be her close collaborators. She wrote me about this venture on October 23, 1977, knowing that I had an interest in pursuing this life of deeper prayer:

> I still do not know how God is going to work in it, and through it, but this is His business. Br. Angelo, the Benedictine, returned to Rome to be one of [the Brothers of the Word].
>
> As for you, I am praying for you, that you do what Jesus wants from you, but wait for the obedience. There is no time for God. That He is calling you it is true, but when and how I do not know. Br. Andrew will give the answer. I wrote a letter to all the brothers to explain. I hope you also got that letter.
>
> Your brother Joseph is very anxious to join the

> Brothers of the Word, so I have sent him to Fr. Bede in the South to make an experience of the Contemplative life before we make another step.

Three days later Mother wrote me again:

> Thank you for your letter of October 18. I am praying much for you and am more and more sure that Jesus wants you to guide and help the little seed of the Brothers of the Word to grow and live. Yes, Brother, I also think the same, they need you.... The small group needs you much.
>
> Don't be afraid; cling to Our Lady. I am praying much for you to her. She will take care of you and the Brothers you will form for her Son.
>
> Pray for me. God bless you.

Mother Teresa wanted me to go to New York straightaway:

> I would like you to spend at least one month in New York with Sr. M. Nirmala. The Parish [priest] will be very happy to have you stay with him. We could then work out the same [constitutions], same life of prayer and proclaiming of Christ. Also Fr. [John] Hardon [S.J.] is there, who knows my mind very well and will help you very much. (From Mother Teresa's Letter to Fr. Sebastian, October 26, 1977)

I felt that I couldn't leave Los Angeles, as I was superior and novice master of seventeen young men. But I did go, with due permission, the following spring. Mother was there too. We discussed the matter of my joining the Brothers of the Word in Rome. Br. Andrew had already granted me the required permission in a letter from Tokyo dated March 3, 1978:

> For years now you have been speaking of a contemplative vocation.... We have talked it over quite a few

times, and I feel there is nothing more or nothing new for me to say now.

Only that I respect your decision, and I know it is impossible to measure what you have been in the life of the Society all these years—not so many years in number, but countless in their intensity and richness.

So I feel that my only reaction can be to accept your decision and to pray that your life may continue to be rich in meaning and inspiration for many others.

You mention mid-June. That is fine. It will be impossible to find anyone to take your place whether it is mid-June or mid-December!

I hope that you will feel that the Society will always have a place for you. Love and prayers.

Men of Prayer

I left the United States on June 1 and reached Rome on June 2, the first Friday of the month and also the Feast of the Sacred Heart that year. On my arrival I found the house to be inadequate for our society. There also seemed to be little sense of direction among the brothers. I wrote Mother Teresa several times. Her reply came later that month:

> God love you for all your letters. Forgive my neglect. If I wrote all the letters I wanted to write to you, you would have got many. Thank God you are at last with the Brothers of the Word. Make sure, right from the beginning, you help the Brothers to be holy. I do not need numbers, but Brothers in love with Jesus, carriers of God's love and compassion.
>
> You know Jesus has used you before as Novice Master; let Him do it again. Only now you have to be a novice yourself in some way. Train them to that deep love for each other. Don't worry about So-and-So's letter [about a delicate matter that caused us pain]; gifts like this I have been receiving many. Just smile and say thank you. I am sure you will soon have all the papers in order.

I am very close to you with my prayer. Let Jesus do with you as He likes.

A few days later Mother sent me a little prayer she had composed:

If we pray—
we will believe.
If we believe—
we will love.
If we love—
we will serve.
Only then we will put our love for God
into living action
Through service to Christ
in the Distressing disguise of the Poor.

At the bottom of the card she wrote:

Thank God for His love for you in giving you to the new Society. Help the Brothers to grow in love and so become Holy, for holiness is the only thing, is the reason of the existence of . . . [the Brothers of the Word].

Though her words were few, her idea was clear. She spelled out succinctly the reason for which God had called the contemplative brothers into existence. She wanted and still wants us to be men of prayer first. A life of prayer stirs into flame the integral gifts of faith, hope, and charity, which are made more and more fruitful in service to Jesus Christ in the poorest of the poor. Growth in love will lead us to greater holiness, which is the sole reason for the existence of our contemplative branch.

Time and again in her letters she wrote, "Be only all for Jesus through Mary." She wanted her brothers to be humble like Mary and holy like Jesus. Like Jesus thirsting on the cross for love of souls, Mother was thirsty for holiness. Her life was an echo of the Beatitudes: "Blessed are those who hunger and thirst for righteousness;...blessed are those who are persecuted for righteousness' sake" (Mt 5:6, 10).

She repeatedly said to the brothers, right from the beginning of my getting to know her, "If you don't want to be holy, pack up and go home. I want men who are in love with Jesus!"

Jesus Living in Us

On August 4, 1981, Mother wrote from Yemen:

> My dearest Brothers, Br. Sebastian and all in Rome,
>
> This brings you Mother's love, blessing and prayer for each one of you that you may grow in the likeness of Christ through love and humility and so proclaim the Holiness of God to all you meet.
>
> You are very much in my prayer—that you really become so free that Jesus may live His life to the full in you.

For Mother Teresa, to proclaim the holiness of God meant to become so free for Jesus that He might "live His life to the full" in us, so that people would see no longer us but only Jesus, who "is the reflection of God's glory and the exact imprint of God's very being" (Heb 1:3). Just as those who saw Jesus were meant to see the Father in Jesus—as He said, "Whoever has seen me has seen the Father" (Jn 14:9)—so anyone who sees the brothers is meant to see no longer them but Jesus. This is exactly what happened with Mother.

She also wanted our community to be like the early Church: "The whole group of those who believed were of one heart and soul," and "they devoted themselves to the apostles' teaching and fellowship, to the breaking of bread and the prayers" (Acts 4:32; 2:42). As she wrote in October 1978:

> Let us thank God for all His tender love for each one of us.
>
> Be "Ek dil–Prempur" (one heart full of love).
>
> Keep the joy of the Lord as your strength—and as a bond of love, peace, and joy with Our Lady and each other.
>
> God bless you. Mother

In the same vein she wrote on June 16, 1979, to the brothers who then formed the Pious Union of the Missionaries of the Word:

> I am sure you will all be happy and willing to make any sacrifice to make your Pious Union another Nazareth—something beautiful for God. You must have much love for each other to be able to forgive, and humility to forget the past. For all is yesterday, tomorrow has not yet come, we all have only today to love Jesus and be holy.
>
> Be one heart, my dear Brothers, only then you can be sure Jesus is with you and you will be able to give Him to others. God bless you.

She gave similar direction to our community in a letter dated August 14, 1979, adding:

> Be one heart full of love with Brother Sebastian . . . . If he makes mistakes, you do not make the mistake if you obey him. Jesus will speak to you through him. Love and obey him, and be one heart with him. This is all Mother asks of you. Pray for me. God bless you.

Ecclesiastical Recognition

Mother Teresa loved the Church and respected and obeyed the magisterium, even blindly. For her the Church was our safeguard, the sure way to know God's will and follow it. She took our Lord's words to the apostles seriously: "Whoever welcomes you welcomes me, and whoever welcomes me welcomes the one who sent me" (Mt 10:40).

She had a very special veneration for the Holy Father: "If he only knew how much his children the Missionaries of Charity love him and how each one of us are ready to give our all to stand by him. Everything of mine is his and for him" (From Mother Teresa's letter to coworker Charlotte Habicht, October 21, 1969).

From the time our contemplative branch came into existence, even when there were just two brothers, Mother Teresa was trying to obtain ecclesiastical recognition. The branch went through some major changes as it developed, which entailed seeking the Church's approval again and again. The main changes consisted of places, name, and habit.

The society began in Rome with the name the Brothers of the Word, which then was changed to the Pious Union of the Missionaries of the Word. Then, on Pentecost Sunday 1985, the Pious Union was renamed the Association of the Missionaries of Charity—Contemplative. On December 8, 1993, our association was elevated to a diocesan religious congregation. Now the official name is the Missionaries of Charity Brothers Contemplative.

Not only was the title changed but so also was the location—several times. The society began in San Gregorio al Celio in Rome; then moved to Acilia on the outskirts of Rome, near Ostia, then to Via Carlo Cattaneo, near the main train station—Stazione Termini—in Rome, where it remained for five months; and then finally, on March 8, 1979, to its present premises, Via di San Agapito 8, Largo Preneste.

At first it was a small group of two or three coworkers. There were many comings and goings as the years went by. Trials of all sorts were not wanting either. Every follower of Christ has to take the Red Sea road. The greatest glory in life is the glory that comes from sacrifice. This is also true for entire religious communities led by their superiors. And in the midst of the thick clouds there was always a ray of light leading and guiding.

Mother's Letters

Mother Teresa wrote a series of letters to ecclesiastical authorities—especially to the cardinal vicar of Rome, the prefect of the Congregation for Religious and Secular Institutes, and the Holy Father—requesting approval of the various new names, seeking higher ecclesiastical status or recognition, and so on. She also wrote to civil authorities to seek certain permissions. She always wrote these letters after much prayer, reflection, and penance. Before starting a letter she always made the Sign of the Cross, and she did so again before signing it.

We personally delivered and read these letters to the persons concerned, with great respect and humility but also with peace and joy. Mother's attitude toward all was that she was bringing a simple but beautiful gift to them and to the Church.

Our attempts to obtain ecclesiastical recognition often received negative responses. But I never heard Mother complain, nor did she get discouraged. On the way back from visiting a bishop or cardinal she would say, "Let us pray about it, do double penance, and then talk with the cardinal or the Holy Father."

Mother tried to affiliate our branch to the sisters through Propaganda Fide. Cardinal Poletti gave us a letter of *nihil obstat* to accompany our application, but Propaganda Fide did not think that it was the best solution. I remember Mother Teresa's saying, "Well, that is God's will, I suppose. God has His own way and His own time. Let us keep praying."

One of the main problems was the number of brothers. We were few, and the number normally required to erect a religious institute of diocesan rite is forty professed members.

On June 16, 1993, we met the cardinal prefect of the Congregation for Religious and Secular Institutes. He was delighted to hear that Mother Teresa was starting a contemplative branch of the Missionaries of Charity. He reflected that there are so many religious today who, like the apostles, may work all night long but without Jesus catch nothing. How important it is to pray and to transform the gift of our vocation into a life of prayer!

This is not a part-time job. We are called to pray twenty-four hours each day. From the presence of Jesus in the Eucharist we go to the presence of Jesus in the distressing disguise of the poorest of the poor, and vice versa.

The cardinal called together all the secretaries and all those who worked under him to share with them the great news of our contemplative branch. He led us all to the chapel, where he had Mother start the prayer. It seemed as if the Holy Spirit descended upon us all. We felt heavenly for a little while. The cardinal blessed us, as Mother asked him to do. It was a great morning.

We Meet the Holy Father

From there we went to the Holy Father's office, and Mother read the following letter to him:

> Rome 16.6.93
>
> Our Dear Holy Father,
>
> It was a real gift of God to be present at the Holy Mass with you, to pray with you and receive Jesus from you. Today I come, together with Fr. Sebastian, my cofounder, with good news to offer you a gift.

As you know, the Missionaries of Charity keep growing with God's blessing. We now have Sisters active and contemplative, Brothers, and Priests. Since March 19, 1979, we have the Pious Union known as Missionaries of Charity Brothers Contemplative in the Diocese of Rome. After much prayer and sacrifice, I feel this is the time for the Brothers to become a diocesan Religious Institute. For this I appeal to you to help us, that the Church will grant us this gift.

At present there are 24 Brothers working in Rome, Albania, and Brazil [a house that we closed a few months later]. The very beautiful gift... God has given to the Brothers is to begin the Lay Missionaries of Charity movement for the families. They have already 500 families throughout the world who have consecrated their lives, to live their lives through prayer and the vows of Poverty, Chastity, Obedience and Whole Hearted free Service to the poorest of the poor, as... their married life permits. This consecration has been a very great gift of God to the families. So please, Holy Father, pray for them and bless them.

Father, and I come to you with our whole heart and profound humility, with the help of Mary our Mother, to help us become a diocesan Religious Institute, since this branch is still only a Pious Union. Please, Holy Father, bless your devoted Missionaries of Charity that they become true Contemplatives, fully consecrated to God and His Church so that whatever they do be done for the glory of God and the good of the Church.

Please, Holy Father, pray for Fr. Sebastian and for me.

Your devoted children in Mary,
Fr. Sebastian, Missionary of Charity
M. Teresa, Missionary of Charity

Mother also spoke about the total number of tabernacles the Missionary Sisters of Charity had in over 120 countries of the world. The Holy Father blessed us all and greeted

Mother again and again with great tenderness and affection. "All right, Mother Teresa, all right. I shall see." We were all thrilled to be with him.

Success at Last

We also made a visit to the cardinal vicar of Rome, Camillo Cardinal Ruini, with another letter. He took great interest in our society. He said that our request depended more on the Congregation for Religious and Secular Institutes than on him. If they gave him the *nihil obstat*, he would have no problem. The Office of the Congregation for Religious and Secular Institutes had also asked us to present an updated copy of the Constitutions and several other documents, which needed time and hard work to prepare.

With the help of the Holy Spirit, and with much prayer and penance, the Constitutions and all the other necessary documents were submitted to the Office of the Sacred Congregation for Religious and Secular Institutes by September 1993, and we waited patiently and prayerfully for a favorable reply. We remain ever grateful to the Sacred Congregation for giving the Nihil obstat and to the cardinal vicar for designating the Missionaries of Charity—Contemplative as a diocesan religious congregation on December 8, 1993, adding another chapter to our life and history. Our Lady wanted us to have this gift on the Solemnity of her Immaculate Conception, not only to impart her maternal blessing but also so that every child of our society would resemble her and take her as his Mother and model.

Mother Teresa's role in the founding of our contemplative branch of the Missionaries of Charity is clear. She not only gave birth to it, but she also nourished and strengthened it by her prayer, penance, and motherly care.

Her letters, her talks, and her meetings with the brothers are all proof of her keen interest in us and of, in her own words, "the joy of conviction that the contemplative brothers will be a fruitful branch on the Tree of Life—Jesus" (from Mother Teresa's letter to Br. Sebastian, September 16, 1977).

CHAPTER SIX

CONTEMPLATIVE YET APOSTOLIC

The Missionary of Charity Brothers Contemplative now have houses in Rome, Albania, India, and Ghana. Our motherhouse and generalate is in Rome, where we also have a night shelter for men known as Casa Serena, "peaceful house." It accommodates about seventy men who otherwise would sleep in the open. Not only do these older gentlemen find a warm bed for rest, but they also receive a full meal each evening, besides necessary facilities.

Working with prisoners, visiting the elderly and the lonely, carefully serving the homeless with breakfast on the streets each day—these are also integral parts of the work of our society, often performed with the help of volunteers. We administer the sacraments, especially the sacrament of reconciliation. We give spiritual direction to the Lay Missionaries of Charity and others. Also part of our apostolate are the Eucharistic services and pastoral help that we render to the Missionary Sisters of Charity and the poor they serve. It is a good life!

Our House in Albania

It was on August 15, 1989, that Mother Teresa first set foot on Albanian soil, where rest the mortal remains of her dearly beloved mother Drana and her sister Aga Bojaxhiu. For her it was a shocking experience. Besides the obvious poverty was the interior poverty stemming from the atheism imposed there for years by a totalitarian government. She wanted by all means to send the sisters there.

Three weeks later Mother had a serious heart attack in Calcutta. I visited her and celebrated Holy Mass in her hospital bedroom. As I was leaving she took my hand and told me to "pray to Our Lady to tell Jesus to make Mother all right, so that Mother can take Jesus to Albania." She wanted all of us to pray for this special intention. She seemed like a mother giving birth to a child: Mother Teresa was giving birth in pain to her communities in Albania.

The following spring Mother Teresa again tried to go to Albania, but her "hour was not yet come." Finally, on March 2, 1991, she and four sisters opened their first house in Tirana. She eventually opened one more house in the capital city; one in the seaport of Durazzo; one in Elbasan, the geographical center of Albania; and a fifth one in Shkodra in the Catholic north of the country—thus completing the first five mysteries of the rosary.

At that time Albania had a total population of about three million people. By its constitution an atheist state, it was reduced not only to material poverty but worse still, to spiritual poverty. In the sixties the dictator Enver Hoxha had ordered the confiscation of all the Catholic institutions and churches. The huge Catholic cathedral in Shkodra was turned into a sports stadium. Other churches likewise became sports stadiums, ammunition depots, and other such facilities.

By March 1967 no one was allowed to mention God's name or speak of Him or pray to Him. Priests were arrested, most of them put to death or sent to prison, where they were consigned to forced labor. Many Catholics offered their lives on the altar of martyrdom. Some fled to Italy or to other neighboring countries.

Hoxha totally isolated Albania from the rest of the world, cleverly making Albanians believe that their country was the best in the world and their people the happiest. This sort of brainwashing prevailed until the death of Hoxha in 1986.

Mother telephoned from Tirana toward the end of July 1991, asking for one of our priests to come help the sisters and the poor with their spiritual needs. I was in America at the time, and it was from there that I returned her call. She spoke of sending Br. Piet to Albania.

I said, "Mother, I hear that there are twenty-three Albanian priests there."

"Yes," she said, "but they are old and not updated!"

It was true. When Albania became independent in 1990, there were twenty-three Albanian priests who emerged as survivors of the great tribulations. Practically all were in their sixties or seventies, and their formation and theology were pre-Vatican II. Since they had been totally isolated from the rest of the world, they had no idea of the changes that had taken place, including the liturgical reforms. They had no books, vestments, or other liturgical accoutrements.

Since June we had been examining the possibility of opening a second house somewhere outside Rome. In fact, two of us had gone to meet the Cardinal of Naples, who was ready to welcome us and to give us a beautiful place. Now Albania seemed the right place to go. So Br. Piet went to Tirana on July 31, 1991. Then one of our coworkers, Dr. Giancarlo Velluti, was taking things to the sisters in Albania via ferry, so Br. Luke and I went with him.

We entered Albania at one of its northern border posts, Hoti. The first sight really shocked us. I had never seen a country reduced to such misery. There are really poor people in the so-called third world countries, but if one has money, one can buy whatever one wants. Here there were no shops. We could not even get a cup of water on the main road to Tirana.

We stopped to visit our sisters in Shkodra, who welcomed us very warmly. After a break of a couple of hours we continued our journey to Tirana. We spent a few days there, then returned to Rome for our annual retreat. Spiritually refreshed, two of us and one of our volunteers returned to Albania to look for a house for our society.

We took the same route as previously and reached Shkodra on September 5, 1991. The following day a local priest named Fr. Luigj Çira brought us to the village of Bushat, nine miles south of Shkodra on the Tirana Road. The Catholics of Bushat urged us to establish our community there. All they asked from us was Holy Mass on Sundays, in whatever language.

So on Sunday, September 8, 1991, we returned and celebrated our first Holy Mass in Bushat. The following week more brothers arrived from Rome. We officially inaugurated the community on September 14, 1991, the Feast of the Exaltation of the Holy Cross.

There was much work to do both inside and outside the house. In the following year we undertook the building of a church adjacent to our house, and it was blessed in January 1993 by Archbishop Ivan Dias, the apostolic nuncio for Albania. He told us that it was the first new church to be constructed and blessed in Albania since the end of the communist regime. He made it clear to the people that although the church could be used as a parish church for the time being, they might eventually have to build their own.

Seeing the utter poverty of the people, we decided to concentrate on providing material help. There followed many adventurous trips with trucks and vans, bringing every sort of help to our mission in Albania. Many villages were under our care. The Catholic children, and the Catholic populace in general, were in dire need of catechetical formation. None of us really knew the Albanian language.

Mother Teresa came to Shkodra on April 25, 1993, the day of the Holy Father's apostolic visit, when he consecrated four new bishops for Albania. Mother only greeted us outside our house, as she had to be in Tirana to take part in the farewell ceremony for the Holy Father. However, she promised to return sometime in August, and this she did on August 18, 1993.

After attending Holy Mass, greeting the people, and having breakfast with us in Bushat, Mother wanted to visit Kukel. By then we had taken responsibility for the presbytery and church in this village about six miles east of Bushat. We had rebuilt the church, which is presently used as a parish church, and had begun our novitiate there.

Much has happened since we began our mission in Albania, and more than once our lives were in real danger. On August 26, 1997, twenty-six of us were on retreat in Bushat. We had just finished a midday Holy Mass when suddenly a man of twenty-five came into the church carrying a loaded automatic weapon, with two grenades prominently strapped to his belt. We were dumbfounded. Our only help was God, who is always there when we look for Him. By His grace the man surrendered. Within the hour we resumed our retreat.

This happened to be Mother Teresa's eighty-seventh and last birthday on earth. After the incident I called to wish her a happy birthday, without telling her what had happened a few minutes previously. This was my last conversation with Mother Teresa.

Br. Martin, from Ghana, had a heart attack in Bushat and went home to God on May 27, 1996. He was only thirty-nine years of age. We buried him in Kukel. May he rest in peace.

Although our work in Albania now consists mainly of spiritual, pastoral, and catechetical ministries, we are also building a home for forty handicapped boys in the same area. We still distribute material aid, but only to a few really poor people. We lack any certainty that our physical lives are safe and secure, as there are still occasional shootings.

Our House in India

It was during our novena to St. Joseph in March 1994 that a letter arrived from the archbishop of Agra, inviting us to open a house in his archdiocese. I left for India on April 7 to meet the archbishop and to see what his invitation entailed. He offered us the old cathedral called "Akbers' Church." Unfortunately, neither the place nor the conditions were entirely satisfactory for our way of life.

Visits to the archbishop of Delhi and the bishop of Kalyan-Bombay afforded us other possibilities. After much prayer, reflection, and penance, we cast lots to know in which of the three dioceses to open our new house, and the lot fell to Delhi. Archbishop Alan de Lastic told us we were welcome to open a house anywhere in his archdiocese but not to ask him for anything else.

Returning to Rome, we prayed and discussed the matter, and we decided to make a foundation in the archdiocese of Delhi. The Missionary Sisters of Charity in Jampura, New Delhi, were a great help in finding us a vacant house in the area of Gurgaon, in the state of Haryana, which belonged to the Patrician Brothers of Palam Cantonment. We began in this temporary residence on Sunday, July 3, 1994, the solemnity of St. Thomas the Apostle, the first missionary to India.

We began our community with nothing. We needed a permanent location, volunteers, coworkers, as well as a suitable field of apostolate. We were unable to conduct any business properly, as we were not a registered organization in India. Our beginnings took time, effort, planning, sacrifice, and prayer. Many volunteers helped us, some local ones and some from Italy.

After much prayer and reconnaissance, we finally found our present site. We had completed the land purchase by December 8, 1994, with the help of Our Lady of the Immaculate Conception. In February 1995 we began constructing a small building to house the brothers. The name we chose for the project was *Deepashram,* which means "an oasis of light." May it become a real light! Lord, lead us from darkness to light, from the unreal to the real, from death to immortality.

With God's grace and the help of many people, including the bishop of Chandigarth, Haryana, and the Franciscan Sisters, we were also able to register our society with the government.

On June 26, 1995, a hot and dry Delhi summer's day, the brothers moved to the new premises, although many things still needed to be arranged and completed. A few months later we began to build another and bigger house for the brothers. This house now serves as accommodations for volunteers who come to help the brothers in their work with handicapped boys.

Mother Teresa came in person on November 18 to bless our beginnings. As it was very late and she had had a very busy day, we only wanted her to walk around the ground floor of the new building and bless it with her presence, together with Bishop Vincent Concesao, our auxiliary bishop. But to everyone's surprise, she went upstairs and walked around and saw everything.

During the prayer service Mother thanked the people of Gurgaon and asked them to support the brothers and their work with their prayers, presence, and active cooperation. Needless to say, everyone was happy beyond description, including Mother. Every time she saw me after that she would say, "You have such a beautiful place in Gurgaon, thank God. Make it a real Nazareth, a real place of prayer and of loving service. Make sure right from the beginning you help the brothers to be holy. We do not need numbers, but brothers in love with Jesus, carriers of God's love and compassion."

We now began plans to construct a church, a formation house, and a home for handicapped boys. When these plans were ready, we showed them to Archbishop de Lastic for his blessing, comments, and approval. Then I brought copies of the plans to Rome to show to Mother. On the morning of May 25, 1996, in San Gregorio al Celio, she perused the plans, prayed over them, blessed them, and signed her approval. When she saw the plans for the formation house, she again reiterated the importance of "helping the brothers to grow in love and so become holy":

> For holiness is the only reason for the existence of the Missionaries of Charity. And if the brothers do not want to be holy, let them pack up and go home.
>
> Don't be afraid; cling to Our Lady. My prayers are always with you. Every single Mass I put you in the chalice. For me all of you are one. We are Missionaries of Charity. We are one family. If you need anything please do not hesitate to ask the sisters. We get so much; people are so generous. Thank God. Jesus loves our poor people so much. Now you pray much for Mother, alright.

She signed not only the project but also the reports I had prepared for Missio in Aachen, Germany. This German branch of the Pontifical Mission Societies supports development projects in over a hundred third-world countries. Mother said that Missio would be very happy to help us. They were helping our sisters already, as was the Catholic relief agency Misereor. With the help of innumerable generous people, *Deepashram* is today able to house and look after over seventy homeless, handicapped boys.

CHAPTER SEVEN

THE LAY MISSIONARIES OF CHARITY

In December 1981, a group of coworkers came to see me at our house in Rome. They said that they were fed up with the structured Church and wanted to belong to "the church of Mother Teresa." I had them sit down, and after making some enquiries I realized that they were in need of catechesis.

So we began meeting every Friday from 8:00 P.M. to 10:00 P.M. These meetings were conducted with great liberty and openness. We shared ideas, opinions, and ideals inspired by Mother Teresa and the Missionaries of Charity.

I told them that there is no "church of Mother Teresa." Rather, she was the foundress of a religious congregation approved and recognized by the authoritative Church. If the bishop of Calcutta and Propaganda Fide in Rome had not given permission, she could not have done what she was doing, and the congregation of the Missionaries of Charity would not exist. Mother was a real and faithful daughter of the Church who discerned God's call and responded to Him in and through the Church.

Thirsty for God

For over two years the group met. The number was always on the increase, eventually reaching about twenty-five. From this prayer group there came two men and two women who expressed a desire to belong to the Missionaries of Charity in a closer way, even though they were laypeople. We reflected, prayed, and decided that they could make some sort of vows, although these had to be private. I wrote a formula, named the group "Nazareth Family Movement," and fixed the date of their vows for April 16, 1984, Tuesday in Holy Week, to be made in our chapel in Rome.

I went to see Mother Teresa at the sisters' house in Rome and explained our plan to her. She willingly agreed to come and join us in the celebration of the Eucharist, and she took her place very close to the four who were to make their vows. She had them sign their vow formula on the altar, after which both Mother Teresa and I signed. All were very happy, although we did not know what the future might hold.

After the ceremony Mother, the four professed, and I went to the parish priest, Don Isidoro Del Lungo, and told him of the vows and of the new group in his parish. He gave his blessing, and we came back to our house for some refreshments. With great joy Mother spoke to the brothers of the importance of encouraging families to pray together. And she encouraged all the brothers to persevere in following God:

> If laypeople are so hungry for God, how much more we "M.C.'s," especially you contemplative brothers, should be hungry and thirsty for God. Pray, Brothers, that we may not spoil God's work but remain faithful to our

> charism. . . .
>
> Our poverty is a great gift. For us poverty means freedom. Let us pray to Our Lady. Though she was chosen to be the Mother of God, in her own eyes she was a simple handmaid of the Lord who went in haste to take care of her cousin Elizabeth. There is much to learn from her. You men especially must cling to Our Lady. Pray often, "Mary, Mother of Jesus, be a mother to me just now."

In the next few months there were many enquiries about the new lay movement. Some of us found it difficult to explain to people what it was all about. The name sounded strange to people, as it did not directly and immediately express the adherence of the movement to the family of the Missionaries of Charity. Thus the idea arose to change the name to "Lay Missionaries of Charity."

We wanted to have the full approval and support of Mother Teresa before we did this. We had a long discussion about it with her. On Pentecost Sunday, May 26, 1985, Mother Teresa happily accepted the new name as The Movement of the Lay Missionaries of Charity. Everybody felt happy about this change, as it indicated unity with the whole family of the Missionaries of Charity. It was a real gift of the Holy Spirit on that Pentecost Sunday.

The Lay Rule

Although we now had a better title for the movement, we still did not have any clearly defined statutes for its members. Many members wanted guidelines to follow so they could realize their hearts' desire and quench the thirst of Jesus on the cross, for love of their own souls and of the poorest of the poor, whom they felt called to serve.

We sometimes experience a conflict between our time and God's time. In Greek the word *chronos* indicates "successive time," whereas *kairos* indicates "the appropriate time" or "God's time." Weeks and months passed by. It was hard for me to put the statutes for laypeople into writing, as I am a religious and a priest.

I prayed to the Holy Spirit and to the Holy Family. From September 1986 to February 1987 I devoted most of my time and energy to the writing of the statutes. I struggled, read, and reflected, concentrating especially on the recent teachings of the Church with regard to families—in other words, what our Mother Church expects from and for laypeople today.

To my surprise, I found so much material that I was almost frightened. How many laypeople really live up to the Church's expectations? I wondered. And how many laypeople know their sublime vocation and mission in the contemporary world, where they are called to live and work?

With the Second Vatican Council the Church spelled out clearly and convincingly the universal call to holiness, directed to all men of good will, whether lay or religious. Mother Teresa repeatedly recalled in all her talks that "holiness is no more considered to be the luxury of the few but the simple duty of every Christian." We are duty bound to strive for holiness: "Be perfect, therefore, as your heavenly Father is perfect" (Mt 5:48).

The statutes of the Lay Missionaries of Charity were written in light of this understanding and of the solid teaching of the Church. They propose a high ideal, which may seem beyond the strength of some. In fact, holiness is beyond everyone's power. We all need God's help, which when sought will never be wanting. Jesus knew that none of us would ever reach the heights of perfection He calls us to, yet He wants us to try. We can never think that we have achieved this goal; there is then no room for pride or complacency or discouragement.

We need to proceed step-by-step, holding on to the hands of Jesus, Mary, and Joseph and guided by the Holy Spirit, not by our feelings and fears. Our God is omnipotent—that is, all-powerful. He is omniscient—meaning "all-knowing"—and He is omnipresent, present everywhere. The all-powerful, loving God leaves us for not even a fraction of a second.

So the Lay Missionaries of Charity should have no fear. Jesus is here to help us, to strengthen us, to guide us; and the Holy Family is our model of humility, charity, silence, and prayer. All three persons of the Holy Family are very special. The way they loved each other, the way they helped one another, and the way they grew in holiness were unique and exemplary for all families of the world and especially for Lay Missionaries of Charity of all generations.

Thanks be to God, like any living organism, the Lay Missionaries of Charity also grow and spread, under the shadow of the tree of the cross. They can be found on most continents of the world, in small or large numbers. With God's help and with the assistance of many priests and religious, the already existing groups are growing in holiness and in number; new groups are forming with the help of the Missionary Sisters of Charity and with the guidance of some zealous priests who serve as spiritual directors.

CHAPTER EIGHT

LESSONS IN FAITH

In the Letter to the Hebrews faith is defined as "the assurance of things hoped for, the conviction of things not seen" (Heb 11:1). Abraham, the Father of faith, obeyed God's call to set out for an unknown country (see Gn 12). On September 10, 1946, Mother Teresa heard the same kind of call from God. He wanted her to leave the Loreto convent and set out without knowing exactly where she was going. Abraham and Mother Teresa had one thing in common: "the obedience of faith."

Trusting only in God and in His providence, Mother left Loreto, where she had lived for nineteen years, on August 16, 1948. She was alone and penniless, but she was armed with the power of the Holy Spirit and the spirit of the society she was to found, which is a spirit of total surrender, loving trust, and cheerfulness. Her firm decision, based on the call she had received, was to help the poor. Through her faith God was going to add a new chapter to salvation history and to the history of mankind.

It all began in what, in human terms, appears to be a miserable and even God-forsaken city: Calcutta, with its countless poor living and dying like animals on the streets. Mother Teresa walked out into that ocean of accumulated human misery with the weapons of faith, hope, and charity—with courage and the conviction that the Lord who called her to do His work would give her the means to fulfill it.

It is almost impossible to describe Mother Teresa's profound journey of faith with a few examples. Her whole life was a continual expression of her faith in God's irrevocable promises. Like Our Lady, she trusted. Even in my first meeting with her in 1966, she told me that the work that the Missionaries of Charity do is not their work, nor is it social work. It is God's work. She once wrote me, "I think Jesus wants to prove that it is He and not we, that it is His and not ours. I am very happy with His decision, whatever and whenever it will be."

Jesus' words were "If you have faith the size of a mustard seed, you will say to this mountain, 'Move from here to there,' and it will move; and nothing will be impossible for you" (Mt 17:20). For Mother Teresa faith was that simple. Before her all the doors were wide open, be they those of presidents or prime ministers; of Hindus, Muslims, or Christians; of those with faith or those without faith. Her faith moved many hardened hearts. At times God accomplished through her things that were humanly impossible.

Mother and Our Lady

Mother used to tell people to pray to Our Lady in any grave necessity: "Mary, Mother of Jesus, be a mother to me now." She told me several times to translate this phrase into Italian for people when they came to her with their personal problems. "Is there anything that Our Lady will refuse to us?" she would say. She was spontaneous and natural in flying to Our Lady for help, and after obtaining a favor, she did not take the credit but thanked God and Our Lady.

For Mother Teresa, Our Lady was her mother. In one of her letters to us brothers she wrote, "May she be more and more a Mother to each one of you, for she alone is the way to Jesus, she alone can give us Jesus. So let us continually turn to her with great love" (August 14, 1979).

She recommended the *Memorare*, which she herself prayed often. It was for her a key to many graces and favors, including material benefits. Before approaching any important person, whether ecclesiastical or civil, she would say to us, "Let us make a quick novena to Our Lady." She always added a tenth *Memorare* to thank Our Lady in anticipation of her answer to the request.

Mother promised Our Lady one hundred thousand *Memorares* when she was searching for the present motherhouse. She taught the prayer even to non-Christian children, as she and the few sisters who were with her then were not able to recite them all by themselves. She had reached eighty-three thousand *Memorares* when an old man with a white beard came and asked her whether she needed a house. She said yes, so he took her to the owner of a building and rang the bell. The doorkeeper opened the door, and as she went in, she turned back but did not see the man anymore.

The owner of the building was very surprised, as he had not publicly declared his intention to sell the house. He kept asking her, "But who told you that I have a house for sale?"

She only said, "An old man told me about your house and brought me to you." She did not know what else to say. She was sure that Our Lady had sent St. Joseph to take her to the right person.

Our Lady was her secure refuge and her "confidante" from the very first day of her decision to dedicate herself exclusively and totally to the service of the poorest of the poor. In all her letters and talks she invited us to cling to Our Lady: "Don't be afraid, cling to Our Lady. I am praying much for you to her. She will take care of you and the Brothers you will form for her Son" (From Mother Teresa's letter to Fr. Sebastian, October 26, 1977).

She recited the rosary almost constantly and the Little Office of the Immaculate Conception, part by part, throughout the day. All the liturgical feasts of Our Lord and Our Lady were for her great opportunities to express her love and respect for Jesus and His Mother.

Once she went to the airport with more than fifty-five boxes to take to Calcutta. At the check-in desk the clerks objected: "No, Mother Teresa, there are too many, and you have no permission. We are sorry." She tried to convince them. No way would they agree to her terms.

So she told us all, "Let us start a quick novena to Our Lady." We finished ten *Memorares*, the last one to thank Our Lady in anticipation. But the answer was still negative.

Mother told us to start a second novena. As we reached the eighth *Memorare,* a man came out and said, "OK, Mother Teresa, you may take them all for your poor people in Calcutta."

I was present in December 1979, when Mother Teresa asked the Holy Father if she could open a house for the sisters in the Vatican. Pope John Paul II's reply was "I have to ask my Superiors!"

The house in Primavalle, a popular residential area of Rome, was his answer. On November 1, 1980, the house was inaugurated. But Mother Teresa wanted a house right inside the Vatican walls. She kept praying to Our Lady. And so what seemed impossible in the beginning became a reality. Pope John Paul II gave her permission to have a house right inside the Vatican, which Mother called *Dono di Maria* "The Gift of Mary."

Heroic Faith

Mother's faith fueled her incredible love. In 1981, one of our candidates stood talking for such a long time that many of us became indignant. But Mother Teresa did not. I said to myself, "What an incredible patience!" Mother saw in him the suffering Christ. She repeatedly said, "The more repugnant the person is, the more faith is required to serve him." Many times what I thought was a waste of time she thought of as adoration of Jesus in His own pain and fatigue. One needs heroic faith to act the way she did.

In New York in July of 1984, one of the Missionary of Charity Sisters organized a meeting with Mother Teresa, me, and some Americans who had spent some time with the Missionaries of Charity Brothers Contemplative. They all had left for various reasons. That morning's meeting is seared in my memory. Mother patiently listened to several accusations against me. She did not say much but asked the former candidates:

> Whom did you go to Rome for? For Fr. Sebastian or for Jesus? If you had gone for Jesus, you would have stayed. Because you went for something else, you did not stay. Whoever joins a congregation joins for Jesus. The humble Jesus, the obedient Jesus, the poor Jesus. The superior can be miserable, but Jesus is not.

I could see Mother's deep faith in this answer. I felt as if I were the woman caught in adultery and Mother was Jesus. The ones who had come to stone me dropped their stones and went away one by one.

Mother's life of prayer was exemplary, and she exhorted us all to remain faithful to prayer, especially Mass and eucharistic adoration. Once Mother was scheduled to give a talk at St. Patrick's Cathedral in New York. The cardinal called her one morning to say that some difficulties had been raised by some religious in New York. Mother told the sisters to expose the Blessed Sacrament and pray for those who objected to her speaking. The sisters began adoration straightaway. At 1:00 P.M. the cardinal called again to say that the problem had been resolved.

She often told me to remember her every time I put water in the chalice before the offertory at Holy Mass. Whenever people asked her, "Mother Teresa, could you please tell us where you get your energy?" she always pointed to the tabernacle. One of her favorite Gospel passages was "I am the vine, you are the branches.... Apart from me you can do nothing" (John 15:5).

Faith amid Suffering

Mother Teresa had several crises of health starting in June 1983. The first one put her in Salvator Mundi Hospital in Rome. A second and bigger crisis in September 1989, was in Calcutta, and she was taken to Woodland's Nursing Home. In both places she received permission to have Holy Mass as well as eucharistic adoration in her room. Just as the body needs food for its nourishment, the soul also needs spiritual food.

In each of these crises and in those to come Mother deepened her faith. She used her suffering for the glory of God and for the good of the people. Only once, in December 1996, she told me after Mass in her bedroom, as she was sitting in her wheelchair, "Jesus is asking a bit too much from me." I thought of Jesus' words in the Garden of

Gethsemane: "My Father, if it is possible, let this cup pass from me; yet not what I want but what you want" (Mt 26:39). Mother Teresa's life was a continual "yes" to the Father: total surrender in loving abandonment to God's most holy will. Each sigh, each look, each action, was an act of faith, hope, and love.

Mother Teresa's faith was all this and much more. It was a living and active faith, dynamic and solid. It enabled her to become what she was and do what she did for the greater glory of God and the good of people.

Mother used to say, "When I die and go home to God, I can help you much more." In this she resembled her patron, St. Thérèse, who said, "I will spend my heaven by doing good on earth." Considering all Mother Teresa did during her earthly life, what glorious riches we can expect from her intercession now!

CHAPTER NINE

LESSONS IN HOPE

Mother Teresa's childhood home was her first school of all the necessary virtues, including that of hope. At the age of nine she lost her beloved father, which left a big hole in the family spiritually and financially. But the family's hope did not crumble. They continued in the "confident expectation of divine blessing" (*Catechism of Catholic Church,* 2090).

The *Catechism* says that hope "is also the fear of offending God's love and of incurring punishment" (2090). Mother from an early age took care to please God. If ever she did commit any offense against Him, even a slight one, she insisted on going to confession straightaway. She went at least once a week. She used to say, "The sinner goes to confession with his sins, and the same sinner comes out of the confessional without sin."

In her every letter she speaks of becoming holy. For example: "But my prayer is each day and every day with each one of you, that you may become holy because Jesus your God is Holy" (letter to Fr. Sebastian and Brothers, May 1977).

Relying on the Lord

Lazar's move from home was another sorrow Gonxha endured, just five years after her father's death. Then, at the age of eighteen, she realized that God was calling her to leave her mother and sister, whom she dearly loved, as well as her friends. It wasn't easy for her to travel all the way to Ireland by train, to learn English, and then to travel again by ship for more than three weeks to India. Already she loved Jesus deeply and was willing to face any challenge for His sake.

Later she would suffer her inability to visit her beloved mother and sister in Albania before their departure from this world:

> After a long time I had a letter from Albania. My mother is in the last stage of her journey to God. So we have only a little time more to bear it. The forty-one years of her longing for her child will be answered by Him who alone could ask such big sacrifice from her and her child. (From a letter to Charlotte Habicht, May 10, 1969)

Life in India was difficult culturally and linguistically. When she experienced her second call, she needed still more courage to step out and begin her new campaign of wholehearted free service to the poorest of the poor of the streets of Calcutta.

> I need many graces and much strength from Christ, that I persevere in surrendering—to this blind love which is leading me only to Jesus Crucified. But I am happy, so happy as never before, and I would not give away my suffering for any price.
>
> Don't think that I am only suffering. Oh no, I am laughing more than I am suffering, so that some conclude that I am a spoiled Bride of Jesus who is living with Jesus in Nazareth—far away from Calvary.
>
> I must go—India is hot like hell, but the souls are

> beautiful and precious because Jesus' Blood dewed them. (Written from Loreto convent, February 8, 1937)

Mother lacked everything except faith in the promises of the Lord. At first she could not find a house of her own, and she did not have any followers. She recorded her struggles in her diary:

> When I went round looking for a home, I walked and walked till my legs and my arms ached. I thought how they must also ache in body and soul looking for home, food, help.
>
> Then the temptation grew strong. The palace buildings of Loreto came rushing into my mind—all the beautiful things and comforts, the people they mix with, in a word everything. "You have only to say a word and all that will be yours again," the tempter kept on saying.
>
> Of free choice, my God, and of love for You, I desire to remain and do whatever be Your Holy Will in my regard.... Even if I suffer more than now, I still want to do Your Holy Will. This is the dark night of the birth of the Society. My God, give me courage now—this moment to persevere in following Your call.

The Holy Spirit illuminated her convictions and strengthened her faith, hope, and charity.

The Kiss of Jesus

One time Mother felt from a letter of mine that I was very discouraged. So she wrote:

> Trials and temptations are but the kiss of Jesus, a sign that you have come so close to Him that He can kiss you. Don't be afraid, the little Society has to imitate only its Master. To be able to redeem the world, he accepted Bethlehem, Nazareth, Calvary. You are at present in Bethlehem. (January 17, 1979)

As the Missionaries of Charity began to grow in number, they did not always grow equally in holiness. Mother Teresa couldn't give adequate formation to all the sisters. Vocation crises—lack of conviction in one's irrevocable call from God and failures in perseverance—began to be a problem in the society. Mother, far from being discouraged, encouraged her sisters to pray more fervently against defections, offer more sacrifices, and smile more tenderly. Mother suffered humiliations, trials, and crosses for the society, for the poor, for the sick and the weak, both in body and soul. Her life resembled that of St. Paul:

> Are they ministers of Christ? I am talking like a madman—I am a better one: with far greater labors, far more imprisonments, with countless floggings, and often near death. Five times I have received from the Jews the forty lashes minus one. Three times I was beaten with rods. Once I received a stoning. Three times I was shipwrecked; for a night and a day I was adrift at sea; on frequent journeys, in danger from rivers, danger from bandits, danger from my own people, danger from Gentiles, danger in the city, danger in the wilderness, danger at sea, danger from false brothers and sisters; . . . hungry and thirsty, often without food, cold and naked. And, besides other things, I am under daily pressure because of my anxiety for all the churches. Who is weak, and I am not weak? Who is made to stumble, and I am not indignant? —2 CORINTHIANS 11:23-29

Mother Teresa went through severe trials of other sorts. Particularly tragic was the loss of some of her sisters in road and other accidents. In an airport in Africa, as her plane was preparing for take-off, it hit five people, killing them all on the spot. This included one Missionary of Charity Sister, two children, and two coworkers who had come to see Mother off. Mother Teresa came out of the aircraft and stood there speechless. Everybody was nervous and agitated, but she very calmly took care of the pilot, who was in shock and overcome by feelings of guilt.

Another time she and the bishop of Darjeeling were going to see what the sisters could do for the flood victims of the area. Mother was thrown out of their jeep and received a large gash on her head, which began to bleed profusely. Everyone was worried and anxious, and there was quite a commotion. Mother maintained her typical calm. She held her head tightly and told them to stop crying and take her to a hospital. She had to have eighteen stitches.

When she heard of the death of two of her very dear sisters, Sr. Sylvia and Sr. Kateri, Mother's response was that our community in heaven was growing. She always spoke in terms of "when we die and go home to God," instead of simply "when we die." Her hope included "the confident expectation of . . . the beatific vision of God" (*Catechism of the Catholic Church,* 2090).

On a couple occasions she asked me to anoint sisters who were terminally ill, to prepare them for their eternal beatitude. The way she prepared them for the sacraments made one feel that for her, death was like opening a door to a new and better life. She also made us understand that our future life depended on how we lived our "today."

Spreading Hope

"Discouragement is a sign of pride," Mother used to say. "We must be men of hope." She always had words of encouragement for people:

> It is not success that matters for God but faithfulness.
> Never stop trying.
> God is in everyone.

> "Where there is despair let me bring hope" (From "The Prayer of St. Francis").

Mother would find something good in each person and give him or her the opportunity to exercise that goodness. Once I spoke ill about myself, and she said, "See all the good you do to laypeople. So many are touched by your prayers, sacrifices, and words. God is really using you,"and so on.

She did not worry about yesterday or tomorrow. She often said, "Do what you can, and do it now, and do it well"—that is, wholeheartedly and freely.

People of all walks of life, of all ages, of every social standing and position, went to her. To all she invariably gave miraculous medals and what she called "my business card." On this was written:

> The fruit of silence is prayer,
> the fruit of prayer is faith,
> the fruit of faith is love,
> the fruit of love is service,
> the fruit of service is peace.

"Have you got my business card?" she would ask people—believers or atheists, presidents or simple people. She gave her time, her faith, and her tender charity, and all went away from her with hope.

Mother met a lonely man in Australia. He lived in a dirty room, never cleaned or washed himself, never wanted even to light a candle, as he was so depressed. Mother asked him, if she were to send her sisters to him, would he continue to light the candle they had brought and to remain clean and tidy? He agreed. Two years later, when Mother Teresa visited Australia again, he sent word to her that the candle that she had lit in his life two years before was still burning: the candle of hope, peace, and joy.

Indeed, Mother Teresa was a real candle of hope in this dark world of ours. Millions of people have been brought to hope through her and through the Missionaries of Charity.

> Do not be afraid, Jesus said. Put your hand in His hand and walk with Him all the way. Keep the joy of loving Jesus in your heart, and share this joy with all you meet. (Letter of Mother Teresa to Fr. Sebastian and Brothers, February 13, 1983)

CHAPTER TEN

LESSONS IN LOVE

Mother Teresa lived the commandment of all commandments in an extraordinary way. Her love was never much on the level of theory but always very concrete and practical. It was never halfhearted, tepid, or mediocre but ardent and active. She loved her God with all her heart, soul, mind, and strength.

God Loved Us First

Mother was very aware of God's great love for her and for all people, especially for His poor people. She was deeply attuned to the teaching of St. John the evangelist: "In this is love, not that we loved God but that he loved us and sent his Son to be the atoning sacrifice for our sins" (1 Jn 4:10). Often she would write, "How great is His love for each one of us," or words to that effect.

To describe God's love for us, she liked to use the example of one mother's love for her child. During the earthquake in Armenia in 1988, it happened that this mother and her child were trapped under debris. Though they were not crushed, they could not get out and had no food or water. The mother cut one of her own fingers and fed the child with her blood. When the rescue workers reached them, the mother's condition was already critical, and later she died. This is a story of true motherly love. The mother preferred to save her child, even if she lost her own life.

This is exactly what our God did for us in Jesus Christ. Jesus shed His blood to the last drop in order to save us from sin. He continues to feed us with His Body and Blood. Mother Teresa used to say, "When we look at the cross, we know how much Jesus loved us. He loved us to the very end. But when we look at the tabernacle, we know how much Jesus loves us now."

Jesus revealed His Sacred Heart to St. Margaret Mary Alacoque as "the Heart that has so loved men." Mother freely expressed her gratitude to God for this great love. She wrote in October 1978, "Let us thank God for all His tender love for each one of us."

So We Should Love Him

Mother was always aware that she was working for the King of Kings and that she was His beloved and faithful spouse. "To me Jesus is everything," she used to sing and taught us all to sing. "What is there that I would not do today for love of you, Jesus, my Crucified Spouse?" was always in her heart and on her lips. That is why nobody could stop her. She continually stirred the fire of divine love and the zeal for souls into flame.

From the day of her initial inspiration, September 10, 1946, Mother was profoundly aware of God's intense thirst for souls. In her explanations of the Rule she wrote:

> The aim of our Society is to quench [the] infinite thirst of a God made man. Just like the adoring angels in heaven

who ceaselessly sing the praises of God, so the Sisters [and Brothers], using the four vows of Absolute Poverty, Chastity, Obedience, and Charity towards the poor as their chalice, fill it with their acts of observance of these vows and continually give the thirsting God to drink of their love and of the love of souls they bring to Him. Jesus was thirsty on the Cross on Calvary. So the Missionaries of Charity must always be with Our Lady at the foot of the Cross of Jesus with their chalice lifted right up, as to quench the burning thirst of Jesus.

Jesus says, "I thirst"; the Missionary of Charity should answer, "I'll quench." The quenching will cost a good deal, for to satisfy completely an infinite thirst—it will mean a continual giving, a life of sacrifice. Therefore... our life should be one of giving love—sacrifice to God, that is—of real sacrifices made of our own free will and choice. We quench His thirst—not because we must but because we love.

We must observe our vows with great love and generosity, if we wish to quench this burning thirst of God. The observance of the four vows will make us fervent religious—and fervent religious have a great power over the heart of God. If He rewards the quenching of physical thirst (Mt 10:42), think what will He not do for us, if we try to quench His own thirst—the thirst of His Heart.

Let us always remain with Mary, our Mother—on Calvary near the crucified Jesus with our chalice filled with the wine of self-sacrifice, always held up close to His suffering Heart so that He may be pleased to accept our love and give us love in return.

When I was in Los Angeles, Mother wrote me from Calcutta:

Our vocation is to belong to Jesus, and . . . nothing will separate us from the love of Christ. How great is our vocation. How full of joy and holiness we must be out of real gratitude. (May 1977)

Mother's life was based on this intense and infinite love of God. On her way to the chapel it was her custom to pray silently:

> Each sigh, each look, each act of mine
> shall be an act of love divine;
> and everything that I shall do
> shall be, dear Lord, for love of You.
> (From Mother Teresa's Prayer Book)

Every time she put on her sandals, she prayed, "Of my own free will, dear Jesus, I shall follow you wherever you may go in search of souls, at any cost to myself and out of pure love for you" (from Mother Teresa's Prayer Book). One of her favorite expressions was "Be only all for Jesus through Mary."

Her love for Jesus in the Eucharist was unique and profound. She understood very personally Jesus' words in the Gospel:

> Those who eat my flesh and drink my blood have eternal life, and I will raise them up on the last day; for my flesh is true food and my blood is true drink. Those who eat my flesh and drink my blood abide in me, and I in them. Just as the living Father sent me, and I live because of the Father, so whoever eats me will live because of me. This is the bread that came down from heaven, not like that which your ancestors ate, and they died. But the one who eats this bread will live forever.—JOHN 6:54-58

This was why she wanted daily Mass, Holy Communion, and eucharistic adoration by all means, even when she was critically ill. If Mother Teresa was able to give life and joy to others, it was because she was in touch with the Source. Her recognition of the greatness of Jesus in the Bread of Life led her directly to the recognition of Jesus in the distressing disguise of the poorest of the poor.

Jesus told the Twelve to watch and pray in order not to enter into temptation. No matter how busy Mother's day was, no matter how sick or weak she felt, she never passed a day without watching at least one hour with Jesus in the Eucharist. In the various hospitals in which she stayed, even those that were not Catholic, she obtained permission to have daily Mass and Holy Communion in her hospital bedroom, as well as adoration. While other people watched television from their sickbeds, Mother Teresa watched with Jesus.

Mother Teresa felt called to consecrate and sanctify herself, the family of the Missionaries of Charity, and the entire world by loving and adoring Jesus in the Eucharist and by loving and serving Him in the poor. She spoke of eucharistic adoration, as well as Holy Mass and Holy Communion, in almost every public talk. "Say often during the day," she wrote us, "'In union with all the Masses being offered throughout the world, I offer you my heart; make it meek and humble like yours.'" When going out for any apostolate, she would repeat this short formula as she entered the car.

Mother wrote to the archbishop of Calcutta in the late forties:

> One thing I request you, your Grace, to give us all the spiritual help we need. If we have our Lord in the midst of us, with daily Mass and Holy Communion, I fear nothing for the Sisters, nor for myself. He will look after us. But without Him I cannot. I am helpless.

All for Jesus

Mother Teresa's fidelity to the spiritual exercises that are enjoined by the Constitutions was meticulous. No matter how late she went to bed—because of all the letters she had to answer and so on—she was always first in the chapel for morning prayer. In one of her instructions she says. "Sisters, for forty years, I have been always first in the chapel. Jesus is waiting for us."

Her love for Jesus had no conditions and no time limits. In all my travels with her I was aware of the constant movement through her fingers of her rosary beads. She practiced the presence of God through the rosary and through ejaculatory prayers. She used to tell me that we should make our resolutions in the morning and then renew them again and again during the day: "All for you, O Most Sacred Heart of Jesus, all for you."

Filled with zeal for souls and burning with the desire to satiate the infinite thirst of Jesus on the cross, Mother Teresa travelled extensively by land and by air. Often without proper rest, exposed to heat and to cold, Mother proclaimed the gospel in season and out of season. People would approach her for spiritual advice, for counsel or help, for an autograph, for a miraculous medal, or for the chance just to touch her. The other sisters sometimes sought to prevent them from coming to her, but Mother welcomed them all with her characteristic smile.

> I long to be only His—to burn myself completely for Him and souls. I want Him to be tenderly loved by many. Self-denial and abnegation will be the means to our end. There will be disappointment, but the good God wants just only our love and our trust in Him

From a human point of view, Mother was doing much more than most people can do or want to do, but she never felt that she was doing enough. She wanted to conquer the whole world for her King; she wanted to satiate the thirst of her Crucified Spouse by bringing souls to Him in every way possible.

The demands of her activities and her long and fatiguing journeys consumed her energy and broke her health, but they did not break her spirit or her apostolic zeal. Each of her health crises was a further step in her fervor and love for God. She echoed her heavenly patron, St. Thérèse of Lisieux, "The sharper the thorns, the sweeter my song shall be." Also like Thérèse, she determined "to do ordinary things with extraordinary love." For every photograph that was taken of her, she asked Jesus to free one soul from purgatory.

The unquenchable fire of love for God that burned in her tender heart took her to countries where many others were afraid to venture. She was a pioneer in her missionary journeys to Eastern Europe at a time when much of it was still under strict communist rule. Armed with spiritual weapons—most notably the rosary and the miraculous medal—she approached the leaders of these countries. Her love for God impelled her to speak to hardened hearts with sweetness, kindness, and firmness. As a result of much prayer, sacrifice, and penance, she was able to open several houses in those countries.

Love for Others

When Mother came to India, she was part of the Sisters of Loreto, and her ministry was teaching. She wrote, "I am a teacher, and I love the work. I am also head of the whole school, and everybody wishes me well here."

But then something awakened in her the love for God's poor, for the forgotten and the abandoned whom she saw on the streets of Calcutta. On September 10, 1946, her intense love of God kindled in her the love of her neighbor. In the recesses of her being an indelible impression formed, never to be wiped out. It was like an anointing, an invasion of the Holy Spirit. Her very life from then on was going to be interwoven in the fabric of the life of the poor.

For Mother Teresa, love of God and love of one's neighbor were inseparable, like two sides of the same coin: "Truly I tell you, just as you did it to one of the least of these who are members of my family, you did it to me" (Mt 25:40). Mother's decision to work with the poor of Calcutta was an expression of her ardent love of God. The means to quench His thirst for souls was by feeding the hungry, satiating the thirsty, sheltering the homeless, clothing the naked, and visiting the sick and the imprisoned (see Mt 25:31-46).

Mother said again and again:

> Our vocation is not to work with lepers or the dying people; no, our vocation is to belong to Jesus. And because we belong to Jesus, like the vine and the branches, we produce fruit and fruit in abundance. As long as the branches remain united with the vine, they are capable of bringing forth fruit in abundance. For Jesus said, "I am the vine, you are the branches.... Without me you can do nothing."

This was the scent of her life. All the good fruit she produced was due to her oneness with Jesus in the Bread of Life, which led her to be one with her neighbor, especially with the poorest of the poor. In this way she hoped to quench the infinite thirst of Jesus on the cross for love of souls.

Heroic Love

Mother Teresa knew what God was calling her for, though at first she did not know how to get there. Her love for God urged her to respond to the needs of the poor instead of blaming government or ecclesiastical authorities. Her first question was not what religion did a person belong to but "What does God want me to do for this person in need?" She loved everyone irrespective of caste, color, or religion. She used to say, "Whatever we do, we do it to someone, and that someone is Jesus."

This applied also to her relatives and to other Missionaries of Charity. She said, "We must love all, but we must fall in love with our own," and, "There shouldn't be any competition in a religious community, except in the practice of charity."

How could Mother find time for everyone? In her, God was at work on earth again in human guise. She represented the invisible God made visible through her heroic charity. St. John's definition, "God is love" (1 Jn 4:8), became concrete in her. She used to say to me, "God wants to show that He is Love. God is Love and compassion."

It is little wonder then that people of all religions, all ages, and every state of life flocked to her. For the Hindus in Calcutta she was an incarnation of one of their goddesses.

Mother received not only the charism to love and serve the poorest of the poor but also the grace and the gift to involve others. Right from the beginning she was assisted by many coworkers and volunteers. Not only did she observe the commandments of God and the laws of the Church, but she continually taught others to do the same, bringing them closer to God. She would often quote Matthew 25:34: "Come, you that are blessed by my Father, inherit the kingdom prepared for you from the foundation of the world; for I was hungry and you gave me food. . . ."

CHAPTER ELEVEN

A WOMAN OF VIRTUE

In all her talks, whether to the brothers or to crowds of people, Mother used to say that God wants us all to be holy. Holiness is not a luxury of the few, she said, but a simple duty for you and for me. She often advised, "Be humble like Mary and holy like Jesus."

My experience with Mother Teresa over thirty years convinced me of the extraordinary manner in which she lived the moral virtues—I would say, to a heroic degree. This was a result of her spousal relationship with Jesus and because she allowed herself to be led by the Spirit. She allowed Jesus to take from her whatever He wanted to take, and she received whatever He gave her with a big smile.

She wanted to resemble Our Lady in the practice of the virtues. If there was any woman worthy to be ordained, Mother Teresa told me once, it was Our Lady, but she did not want to be a priest nor did Jesus ordain her. Our Lady wanted only to be God's handmaid. Mother Teresa gave this answer to Pope Paul VI when he asked her opinion regarding the ordination of women to the priesthood.

"As soon as Mary received Jesus at the Annunciation," she used to say, "Our Lady went in haste to her cousin Elizabeth to do the ordinary works." So Mother Teresa, after receiving God's inspiration on September 10, 1946, sought to be God's handmaid, to bear the fruit of Jesus in the real world of men.

Humility

The virtue of humility was a source of strength for Mother Teresa and a means to become holy. She used to say,

> It is easier to understand the greatness of God, but it is very difficult to grasp the humility of God. How could such a great God come into the womb of Our Lady? Here we see God's humility and His poverty.

Mother stressed the importance of humility in our community life. "You must have much love for each other to be able to forgive and humility to forget the past," she wrote us in 1979. Her salutation in a letter to us in 1981 read:

> This brings you Mother's love, blessing and prayer for each one of you, that you may grow in the likeness of Christ through love and humility and so proclaim the Holiness of God to all you meet.

Mother used to say that the way to humility is through humiliations: "Whenever you have a chance to be humiliated, grab it." The last talk she gave to us in Rome, on July 19, 1997, was on humility. She said that only through the joyful acceptance of humiliations would we become humble, and unless we are humble we cannot obey. Jesus could obey His Father even unto death, death on a cross, because He was meek and humble of heart. "Learn from the heart of Jesus to be meek and humble through humiliations, contradictions, and accusations" was one of her last words to us.

There were people who disliked her or her ways of doing things. Some criticized her for the strictness of the rules for the sisters; others, for her conservative ideas and attitudes. She faced those problems with prayer and penance and went on with her work.

Once I saw a priest humiliating Mother Teresa in front a crowd of people. Mother was more concerned with expressing compassion toward him than with worrying about her own hurt. She suffered a lot because of that person, and he took up much of her precious time. She never showed irritation or anger toward him. She tried to help him when he asked. Mother used to say to me, "Remember, he too is one of the poorest of the poor.... He is Jesus in disguise."

Some ecclesiastical authorities questioned her method of doing charitable works. They felt that she was "spoiling" the poor by giving everything freely. They suggested she stop spoon-feeding people and instead help them to help themselves. Other people voiced this same criticism of her work through the years.

Mother's answer was simple. First of all, she said that God was "spoiling" the Missionaries of Charity by providing things freely for the poor; and what we receive freely in the name of the poor we give freely to them. For Mother Teresa justice and charity went hand-in-hand. If God demanded only justice without charity and mercy, we would have already disappeared from the face of the earth.

Secondly, Mother Teresa said, the Missionaries of Charity feed, shelter, and clothe those who are not able to do these things for themselves. This is only a part of what is necessary. Others have a vocation to help people stand on their own feet and work for themselves. There is plenty of work for everybody in this world. We try to do our part of the work, and that is enough for us.

Mother Teresa used to say:

> We are not called to do big things, but small things with great love, ordinary things with extraordinary love, like Our Lady, who went in haste to take care of her cousin Elisabeth. Our Lady did not do great things. She said, "The Almighty has done great things for me." We must be humble enough to recognize the work of the Almighty in us.

Mother had no pretensions about herself. When she went to see an important person, she did not presume that her name would command respect: rather, she prayed ardently, making quick novenas to Our Lady.

People would ask, "Mother Teresa, who will be taking your place after you?"

"Allow me to die first," she would say. But then she would add:

> If God can find someone as miserable as me, although He could never find anyone more miserable than I am, He will appoint her as He did me. It is He and not we, it is His and not ours. So we need not worry at all about tomorrow, but just live today as best as we can. Yes, yesterday has gone, tomorrow we do not have yet, all we have is today, and let us live it well for His glory.

If somebody praised her, Mother would say straightaway, "Thank God; let us thank our Lady." All the attention she received—the crowds flocking to her, the honorary doctorates, the national and international awards, including the prestigious Nobel Prize—did not affect her as a person. She remained humble and simple and available. She would say, "It is all His work." Often she instructed us "to remain always on the ground; and not to let anything, honor or dishonor, praise or blame, humiliations or false accusations, separate us from Jesus."

After all, she was the spouse of the Suffering Servant. She worked tirelessly to make Jesus happy and to console Him by bringing souls to Him. Her favorite passage was "I am the vine, you are the branches" (Jn 15:5). Her perfect and unconditional union with the Crucified Savior was the secret of her life, her work, and the fame and publicity she received.

Mother tried to be available to any person who wished to see her. If she happened to be a little late for an appointment, she apologized straightaway, even if it was not her fault.

For Mother Teresa, humility was not a concept to be defined and explained but the stuff of everyday life, following the example of Jesus, Mary, and Joseph. Mother saw herself and the society she founded as a continuation of Jesus' redeeming work in the world. "The Society has to imitate only its Master to be able to redeem the world."

Patience in Suffering

Mother Teresa considered her major physical crises part of the redemptive work of Jesus. In them she came to see her oneness with her beloved Spouse, crowned with thorns and crucified. Beginning in June 1983, she suffered much in body, and this continued till the day she went home to God, September 5, 1997.

In the later years Mother Teresa began to lose her memory, which became a problem and at times a cause of humiliation. One time in Delhi, India, after we had had Holy Mass together with the sisters, we sat down to discuss the possibility of opening a new house of our contemplative branch. After we had talked for about half an hour, she told me to come back in the afternoon so that we could make further arrangements. In the meantime she said that she would make enquiries, and I should do the same.

In the afternoon I went back as she had asked. I told her of my morning's search and the possibilities it had brought to light. Mother became indignant and said, "You should have talked these things over with me beforehand. Why didn't you come earlier to talk to me, Father? Please don't do things like this."

I was completely taken aback to hear her speak in this way. Then I realized that Mother Teresa had forgotten our morning meeting. When I reminded her of what we had discussed that morning, she looked at me with almost a look of guilt and said, "Oh, Father, forgive me. Perhaps I forgot about it. My memory, my memory. I am very sorry." I myself felt very humbled by her willingness to acknowledge her fault, which was not really a fault at all.

In December 1996 the breakdown of her health came to a climax, and people the world over were concerned about her condition. Mother Teresa looked sad and downcast. It was clear to those who knew her that her spirit was passing through thick clouds, and the devil was trying to take advantage of her weakened condition. As I was taking leave of her one December morning, after Holy Mass in her hospital room, she told me in a very low voice, "Jesus is asking a bit too much."

It seemed to me as if her beloved Jesus was reliving His agony in her, in order to redeem the world anew from the darkness of sin. Her hands became blue, as if she were bearing the wounds that the nails had left in Jesus' flesh. Just as "by his bruises we are healed" (Is 53:5), so now in her wounds, in her pain, we were healed and comforted.

After all the hardships and sacrifices Mother Teresa had endured for years for her beloved Spouse, one might have expected a more serene and tranquil end. But instead there she was, a woman of sorrows, bearing not only her own pain but also the burdens of the society and of the poorest of the poor.

Mother Teresa bore it all very humbly. In her Jesus relived His prayer: "My Father, if it is possible, let this cup pass from me; yet not what I want but what you want" (Mt 26:39). The world still needs faithful, zealous, and fervent coredeemers. Mother was chosen to be one of these through the sacrificial love she expressed in words and actions, in her body and in her soul.

Prudence

According to St. Thomas Aquinas, "Prudence is right reason in action." In this sense it can be said that Mother Teresa always practiced the virtue of prudence. She made her decisions "after much prayer and sacrifice," as she often said, as she wanted them to be made according to God's will. She knew the Scriptures well, especially the Gospels, and meditated on them every day.

Our Lady was her model in the practice of this virtue. By nature Mother was timid and very sensitive, but with Our Lady's help she overcame this by prayer, reflection, meditation, and examination of conscience.

For example, when she received the inspiration to begin her new way of life, she consulted the right people, took their advice, and waited for the right moment to act. She knew that there is a time for everything. She took two years for prayer, reflection, and consultation, then, with due permission, left the Loreto convent on August 16, 1948.

But instead of going to work in the slums straightaway, Mother went to the Medical Mission Sisters in Patna, Bihar, for training in elementary medicine and first aid. During the three months she was there, she discussed her ideas for a religious lifestyle, the practice of poverty, and service to the poor with the mother superior. Mother integrated this mother superior's valuable advice into the life of the society when she wrote the Constitutions.

Mother always discussed important matters with higher authorities in order to discern the will of God. She was eager to open houses outside Calcutta before there were enough professed sisters. The archbishop told her to have patience and prepare the sisters properly before she founded new communities. Thus, the first group of sisters received solid formation before they were sent to mission houses. The solidity of a congregation depends a lot on how its members are formed.

One time she was very anxious about the many calls she was receiving to speak in various countries. It happened that Mother and I and a few sisters went to a Holy Mass with Pope John Paul II in his private chapel. After the Mass the Holy Father greeted us one by one. And then Mother told him that she would like to ask him something personal. So they sat down and talked together for a few minutes while we waited.

Afterward she told me that she was at peace, because the Holy Father told her to be at peace and to continue to proclaim Jesus to the people, as they were hungry for God. He told her that she should accept invitations to speak in public, because people would listen to her. So she obeyed the Holy Father.

Mother Teresa's prudence was very evident in all her undertakings, big and small. From the sisters she demanded strict observance of the Constitutions, but at the same time she showed them much love and tenderness. She worked alongside civil and ecclesiastical authorities, while retaining her independence and autonomy. She did not waste her time looking for someone to blame, but she used her gifts to transform the world into a better place, more human and pure.

Discernment

Every time we approached some major decision, Mother required prayer, reflection, and real sacrifices so that God's will would be clear to us and so that we might follow it faithfully and perseveringly. When our contemplative brothers were still a pious union, I asked Mother Teresa if we could try to obtain recognition for a higher ecclesiastical status. She straightaway said yes, let us try. But she told us to pray and sacrifice for three days, and then we would take time together to formulate the letters and go to the Holy Father, the cardinal prefect of the Congregation for Religious and Secular Institutes, and the cardinal vicar of Rome.

An expression she used often was "We must find ways and means to do things." She always had a way to get things done. It was clear that the Holy Spirit was guiding her.

With regard to discerning the machinations of the devil from the movement of the Spirit, Mother followed the example of St. Francis of Assisi and St. Ignatius Loyola. These acknowledged St. Paul's dictum, "Satan disguises himself as an angel of light" (2 Cor 11:14). The evil one is smart enough to make bad things look good, even to pious people. Mother warned the brothers to be attentive in order not to be deceived by the evil one.

For instance, when a religious is happy, by and large, and doing quite well in his vocation, the devil can become jealous and try to disturb him. He might suggest the brother increase his penances without proper guidance or due permission, so that he is brought to the point of discouragement. Or the devil might put into his head the idea to try another kind of religious life. Many of our brothers have been deceived like that and have lost their vocation. This is one of the most common tricks of the devil.

To counteract this snare, she would ask a brother so inclined to wait for one full year, living his present vocation as well as he could. During this period he should not waste his time thinking about other forms of life but rather concentrate on the one he had already chosen. Many sisters to whom she said this did not even write back to her a second time, she said.

CHAPTER TWELVE

THE EVANGELICAL COUNSELS

Mother Teresa's practice of the three evangelical counsels—poverty, chastity, and obedience—flowed like a channel of grace from the Source and Fountainhead of Love, the Holy Trinity. "Our vocation is to belong to Jesus, and nothing will separate us from the love of Christ. How great is our vocation. How full of joy and holiness we must be out of real gratitude" (from Mother Teresa's letters to Fr. Sebastian and Brothers, May 1977).

Mother Teresa kept a very careful watch over her heart and soul, just as she did over her senses. From the first time I met her I was struck by the way she talked and behaved. In her conversations she always showed real love and concern. I never heard her ask a question to satisfy her curiosity. She was careful not to offend anyone by her words or actions. She used to tell me that the Holy Spirit gave her the right word to say at the right time.

Poverty

From the very beginnings of the Society of the Missionaries of Charity, Mother Teresa sought to identify with Jesus. She practiced the traditional penances:

- in imitation of Jesus
- in solidarity with Jesus scourged, crowned with thorns, and crucified
- in solidarity with Jesus in the distressing disguise of the poorest of the poor
- in reparation for her own sins and those of others
- as a mortification—that is, to deprive herself of something she had a right to or that was precious to her, for the love of God
- and as a means for daily conversion
- from the natural to the supernatural—in order to do everything solely for the love of God
- from a life of sin to a life of grace
- from mediocrity to a life of fervor and generosity
- from pride to humility by means of humiliations, to the extent that she desired to be identified with her Spouse Jesus, "the Man of Sorrows"

The lifestyle she chose for herself and for the congregation was simple and austere for two reasons: first of all to identify with Jesus, that others might become rich out of that poverty. This type of poverty is an effective witness to the truth of the gospel. The second reason was because of the kind of apostolate the congregation was called to undertake. They wanted the poorest of the poor to feel at home with the Missionaries of Charity.

The food was very simple but sufficient to sustain the members to do their difficult work. Many times I observed Mother at table. She ate very naturally, without making any fuss and without choosing. She picked up small particles of bread from her plate, as a priest would do from the paten after Holy Communion. For her food was sacred; she knew that many people die each day because of malnutrition or starvation.

Once I was travelling with Mother Teresa from San Francisco to Chicago—just five of us on a private flight. I wasn't feeling too well, so I didn't want to eat. Mother Teresa started filling my plate with all sorts of things. "Today we have and we eat what we have," she said. "Tomorrow we do not know."

Mother had just three sets of clothes, one of which was used only on Sundays and special occasions. Once we were walking through the central part of Rome, and seeing all the shops with fine dresses on display, she said, "Thank God, I do not need any of those things." She always wore sandals, and none of the sisters had wristwatches.

The sisters slept in dormitories and used materials that others would not use because of their poor quality or coarseness. Even when Calcutta was at its hottest, the only fans were in the parlor, for the comfort of visitors, and in the chapel, for the sake of the priests who came to celebrate Mass. There was no stipend, salary, or pocket money for Mother or the sisters. She used the cheapest means of travel possible.

"Poverty must become more and more your joy, freedom, and strength," Mother wrote us on November 8, 1979. "The call is always to follow Jesus, who became poor for us in order to make the poor rich; that is, He emptied Himself, taking the form of a servant to save us."

She depended totally on Divine Providence, and God always took care of her, of the sisters, and of the poor they served. Materials and money poured in, together with much applause and not a few accusations. Mother Teresa used material things as a means to know, love, and serve God. She accepted all help, whether much or little. She saw all she received as God's gift to the poor.

Many times Mother gave us beautiful things: a monstrance, a chalice, a statue of St. Thérèse of Lisieux, one of Our Lady, and many other gifts, both small and big. If people gave her a donation in cash or in kind while she was visiting us, as a rule she would leave it with us. She always said, "If you need anything, please have the humility to ask. We share whatever we have. Freely we received."

Mother remained focused on what she was called to do, strong in her convictions and her spirit of poverty. She used to say, "We must cling to Jesus, and nothing else. Nothing and nobody must separate us from the love of Christ. Nothing and nobody must come between Jesus and us."

Poverty freed her to love her crucified Spouse and to serve Him in the distressing disguise of the poorest of the poor. She emptied herself in order to become the abode of the Blessed Trinity. She knew that the life she lived was no longer her own but that of Christ, who lived in her (see Gal 2:20). The poorer she was, the more closely she resembled Jesus.

Chastity

When we speak about chastity, it is necessary to distinguish between interior and exterior chastity. Of course, certain conclusions can be drawn regarding a person's observance of chastity from his or her manner of dress and mode of conduct. These flow from an interior chastity, an unconditional fidelity to the Lord Jesus.

Mother frequently stressed in her instructions to the sisters the importance of the vow and virtue of chastity and the means to keep it unblemished. Any offense against chastity, however slight, she considered an infringement on the spousal relationship with Christ. As a married woman is to be faithful to her one and only husband, so a professed religious is to be meticulously faithful to Jesus, the beloved Spouse of consecrated souls.

"We have made a vow of chastity, and it is our lifelong fidelity to Jesus, our Crucified Spouse," she would say. Her behavior flowed from this inner conviction of utter fidelity and loyalty.

One reason for introducing the traditional forms of penance, such as the discipline and chain, was to curb passions, which otherwise can get out of control. Mother Teresa avers to this in instructions that she gave to her sisters over the course of the years. She spoke of angelic purity as the aim of every Missionary of Charity. Often she quoted the Beatitudes: "Blessed are the pure in heart, for they will see God" (Mt 5:8).

Mother spoke of Our Lady's heart, "so pure, so immaculate, so full of love and humility." She wanted to resemble Our Lady in this all-important and angelic virtue of purity. One of the reasons she was able to see Jesus in all those she came in contact with was her purity of heart: Her heart was like transparent glass.

Often in her talks to the sisters and brothers she mentioned the example of St. Maria Goretti. She pointed out that "Maria Goretti did not know her catechism lesson, but she became not only a saint but a martyr of purity. Sin, no: death, yes." Every Missionary of Charity must be ready to be a martyr of purity like St. Maria Goretti.

As a rule, Mother Teresa took a partner with her wherever she went, and she demanded that her sisters follow this practice. The religious habit she chose was simple and modest.

She never ate outside or took anything from the places or families she visited, whether rich or poor, lest she develop some subtle attachment. The way she greeted people was the respectful Indian way—with hands joined and a bow of the head, which means, "I honor the presence of God in you." She would not embrace or kiss a person.

One day a priest asked Mother Teresa if he could embrace her just once. I could see her reluctance to comply with his request. However, since he was a priest, she let him do so. She blushed and looked mortified.

As far as I know, people never accused Mother Teresa of any infringements on chastity. She gave no occasion for people to think such things, because her dealings with all were upright, just, and correct. She respected others, seeing the face of Jesus in each person, so others respected her as well.

Obedience

Obedience to the will of God through legitimate superiors was at the heart of Mother's religious vocation. When I was still with the active brothers and told Mother Teresa of my desire to consecrate myself to a more prayerful way of life, she wrote:

> I am glad you spoke to Br. Andrew re your desire to give yourself to contemplative life. Just to make sure that it is the will of God for you, we will pray—and let Br. Andrew decide.... For with the blessing of obedience we can do all things. (From Mother Teresa's letter to Fr. Sebastian, August 8, 1977)

Later she would encourage the brothers under me to the same spirit of obedience:

> My Brothers, make your Community one heart full of love, another Nazareth where Jesus can come and rest a while with you. I know you will make any sacrifices, for this is the test of your love for Christ in the distressing disguise.
>
> My prayer as small as it is, is very very close to you. Help each other to grow in holiness. Be one heart full of love with Brother Sebastian, who even if he make mistakes, you do not make the mistake if you obey him. Jesus will speak to you through him. Love and obey him and be one heart with him. This is all Mother asks of you. Pray for me. God bless you. (Letter to the brothers, August 14, 1979)

Mother Teresa's submission to ecclesiastical authorities was always evident. Several times I went with her to see bishops and cardinals for one thing or another. When she heard that the Lay Missionaries of Charity had been officially recognized by Cardinal Poletti, she was radiant. She asked for copies of the statutes and spoke about them everywhere she went, including to the king and queen in Belgium and in Spain. She gave them copies of the statutes and asked them to contact me.

Prior to the cardinal's approval, Mother had scarcely mentioned the Lay Missionaries of Charity. The Church's recognition was a sign that God wanted them to exist and to spread. She wrote us on January 31, 1990, "Tell the L.M.C. that they are in my prayer daily. We have a light burning for them also at Adoration."

Here I could see how prudent, careful, and patient Mother was before acting or saying yes or no to something that wasn't crystal clear. No one can claim to be doing God's will unless he is ready to obey all legitimate human authorities. To know God's will requires not only time and patience but also much prayer and many sacrifices. We must be ready to walk through life's dark valleys trusting fully in the guidance and assistance the good God gives us to reach the goal to which He calls us. No matter how holy we might think we are, we still need to listen to God in the silence of faith. In fact, the holier we are, the more obedient we are. "To obey is better than sacrifice" (1 Sm 15:22).

Two days before our Constitutions were approved by the Church and our contemplative branch was erected as a diocesan religious congregation, Mother Teresa wrote on the last page of a copy of the Constitutions:

> Come to know
> to love
> to live
> this Constitution, that are
> the written will of God,
> sure way to holiness.
> God bless you.
> M. Teresa M.C.
> Rome 6/12/93

For a Missionary of Charity to become holy, he or she must of necessity cherish a spirit of fundamental obedience to the Constitutions. Mother Teresa was herself an example of this. She tried to live the Constitutions as faithfully and as obediently as she could, and she demanded the same of all her Missionaries of Charity.

Mother Teresa asked me several times to help certain sisters who were unwilling to listen to her or to accept her orders. But the only guidance she gave me was "Try to convince Sister So-and-So of the greatness of her vocation, without accusing or finding fault with her."

One day when she was in Rome, she telephoned to tell me of a sister who refused to be transferred. She had been a professed sister for many years. If she were obliged to move, then she would simply leave the society, she said. Mother Teresa had her come to Rome and tried to convince her of the sublime beauty of her vocation, but it was in vain.

When Mother asked me to talk to the sister, her attitude was not one of finding fault or trying to accuse but rather of trying to help her understand. Her words were always measured, weighed before the Lord. Her uninterrupted union with her crucified Jesus made her both deeply mortified and deeply understanding.

The Fourth Vow

The fourth vow of wholehearted free service to the poorest of the poor was the outlet for the love and grace that Mother received. This service flowed out of her into the lives of millions of people around the world. This was an inner necessity for her: The more she received from the Source of love, peace, and joy, the more she shared with the needy; and the more she shared with the last, the least, and the lost, the more she received. She could be compared to a water tank, receiving through one pipe and then supplying what it has received through another pipe.

Right from the beginning Mother felt the intense and infinite thirst of God in Jesus Christ for the love of souls. She knew well that her mission and that of the Missionaries of Charity would be to quench this thirst. Love for love, love with love. They would do this through the profession of the evangelical counsels and the fourth vow of service to the poorest of the poor. She would state:

> We are the only Congregation that binds its members with a vow of serving the poor wholeheartedly and freely. This vow clearly spells out our distinct vocation to serve exclusively the poorest of the poor. This is specific to the Missionaries of Charity.

In the beginning of her ministry, Mother Teresa's whole attention was on those who were materially poor. Working with Mother for the poorest of the poor, I saw the value and dignity that she saw in each person. Each one was "Jesus in the distressing disguise of the poorest of the poor."

"Jesus cannot deceive us," she used to say. The same Jesus who said, "I am the Bread of Life," is the one who said, "As long as you did it to the least of my brethren, you did it to Me." This was her constant teaching. In her television interview with Malcolm Muggeridge in April 1969, she said, "I want to give to the poor purely for the love of God those things that the rich can get with money."

She claimed every sort of person whom nobody else wanted. She told people in government to contact her if there were unwanted persons. In Calcutta, the government did not want the numerous poor women to be in the jails, so Mother Teresa found homes for them. She set up homes for AIDS victims, as she saw them as the most rejected members of society today.

In her homes for the dying Mother approached people with due dignity, love, and tender care. "They lived like animals on the streets," she said, "but now they can die like angels." She used to say that just as the priest handles the Body of Christ at the altar, so we who receive His Body must treat the broken bodies of the poor with the same respect and reverence.

Whenever there were natural calamities—such as the floods in Bangladesh; earthquakes in Guatemala, Armenia, and India; and droughts—Mother went in person if possible, taking a few sisters with her. She rushed to places affected by war, such as the refugee camps in the 1970s in the north of West Bengal. If she was prevented from going herself, she tried to send sisters, as well as organize help through various social and charitable organizations.

A Deeper Poverty

Yet Mother took man in his totality, seeing not only his bodily needs but also the psychological, spiritual, and moral ones. So serving the poorest of the poor meant serving all their needs, spiritual and material:

- to feed the hungry, not only with perishable food but also with the Word of God, prayer, and the sacraments
- to give drink to the thirsty, not only water but also knowledge, truth, justice, peace, love, and joy
- to give shelter to the homeless, not only providing a house made of bricks but a heart that understands, protects, and loves
- to clothe the naked, not only with a piece of cloth but also with human dignity
- to visit the infirm, crippled, and blind, not only those afflicted in body but also those afflicted in mind and spirit
- to visit the imprisoned, not only those imprisoned behind iron bars but also the ones imprisoned in their passions, selfishness, sin, indifference, and ignorance
- to bury the dead, not only corpses but also bad habits, sins, and selfishness

In every home for the dying, in soup kitchens, night shelters, and children's homes, she made sure that people had the opportunity to pray. When possible, she offered catechism to the poor children of Catholic parents. She consecrated their homes, especially in the month of June, to the Sacred Heart of Jesus. She encouraged families to pray the rosary and parish priests to have weekly hours of adoration with the people in their parishes, along with the sacrament of reconciliation. She organized days of prayer and retreats for the poor and for Catholic families.

As the years went by, she came into contact with the Western world, where she discovered a poverty that was deeper. "To help the poor in Calcutta was easier than to help the poor of the West," she used to say. And she was called to respond to both.

Strongly and emphatically she spoke against the "curse of abortion," which she described as "the biggest destroyer of peace." If a mother can kill her own child, what will there be left in the world? The Missionaries of Charity fight abortion by adoption and by providing homes for unwed mothers. The sisters have these sorts of homes all over the world.

The stance for life requires courage, yet its rewards are priceless. There was a woman who was expecting her fourth child, and the doctors told her that she had a cancerous uterus. She needed an immediate operation, which would mean automatic termination of her pregnancy. I spoke with Mother Teresa about it, and I asked her to write a few lines to the lady. She willingly did this, and she also gave me a miraculous medal to send to the woman. I enclosed these in a letter of my own and offered up many prayers and sacrifices.

The woman decided not to have the operation but to leave the matter to God's tender care and loving providence. Lo and behold, she delivered the baby safe and sound, and there was no trace of the cancer anymore!

Afterword

Through her life and work Mother Teresa gave visibility to the invisible God, as a light bulb makes electricity visible. As the light bulb does not produce the electricity, so too the power to do good belonged not to her but to the Lord. There were therefore no grounds for her to be proud. It was clear to her that the more united she was to Jesus, like the branch to the vine, the more abundantly she would bear fruit for Him.

"Let us thank God and Our Lady" was her spontaneous response when people thanked her for the blessings they received through her prayers. Aware of the Source of all power, she wrote in the first pages of her handwritten Constitutions:

> It was Jesus Christ on the Cross through His blessed Mother—in His great mercy and love—who chose one of His most unworthy and most incapable of human beings to start His own work among the poor. Therefore the Society as a whole or in detail is completely and will always remain the sole possession of the Mother of God.

Jesus redeemed the world. But He calls people to carry on His work of redemption in the world. Mother Teresa was chosen to help the world recognize the presence of Jesus under the distressing disguise of those broken in body and soul. Her invitation to become holy was a pleasant appeal to hearts: "God wants us all to be holy. In the evening of life when we appear before God, we are going to be judged on love."

The task God entrusted to Mother Teresa, though difficult, was very important: namely, to surrender herself totally to His holy will and to dedicate her life entirely to the service of the poorest of the poor on the streets of

Calcutta. According to her, "This was an order." With the command he also gave her the assistance of the Holy Spirit. For her the "Upper Room" was the passenger compartment of a train headed for Darjeeling in the dark hours of the night of September 10, 1946. The gift that she received on that night unfolded with time.

Mother Teresa was given the grace to understand that

> the biggest disease in the world today is not leprosy or tuberculosis, but rather the feeling of being unwanted, uncared for, and deserted by everybody. The greatest evil is the lack of love and charity, the terrible indifference towards one's neighbor who lives by the roadside and is assaulted by exploitation, corruption, poverty, and disease. . . . Only in heaven we will see how much we owe to the poor for helping us to love God better because of them.

Mother Teresa's joy was an expression of God's loving presence in her. "Joy is prayer. . . . Joy is love. . . . Joy is a net of love by which we can catch souls," she wrote in the sisters' Constitutions. I often marvelled at her untiring energy, her calm, and her charming smiles. I saw people come to her with frowns and scowls and go away with radiant faces. Many even confessed their sins to her, and these she directed to a priest for sacramental confession. She had the gift of touching hearts with peace, of anointing them with "the oil of gladness" (Ps 45:7).

Mother Teresa's work disturbed the consciences of many and moved even the most hardened hearts. I have seen politically potent people kneel to kiss her feet. Often her appearances required police protection and even military assistance because of the crowds. When she was sick and stooped, people of all ages and walks of life still ran to her. Many just wanted to touch her feet or her sari, to get her blessing or even just a glimpse of her aged, smiling face.

It was the firm belief of countless people throughout the world that Mother Teresa was a "living saint of our time." Not only Roman Catholics but people of all religions and denominations considered her sanctity heroic, her spiritual gifts extraordinary. The Hindus in India believe that she was another manifestation of one of the goddesses of charity.

The popularity and the formal recognition she received from the most prestigious quarters did not make any difference to her personality or her behavior. Her lifestyle remained simple, humble, joyful, available, ready to serve rather than to be served, ready to do any sort of work. One day she could be with the president and leading ministers of India, and the next she could be found washing and feeding people in one of her homes for the poor. This constancy, this heroic humility and charity, convinced the world of her exceptional holiness of life.

Her photos were distributed by the thousands. Her simple words were quoted at gatherings of the mighty. Her letters and autographs are treasured with meticulous care. Audiocassettes, videos, books, and articles are sold not only in Catholic bookshops but in other religious and nonreligious venues. Many of these items can be found in various languages, even some of the less spoken languages of the world.

The years of selfless and dedicated service in no way diminished her initial fervor, her heroic charity, her zeal for the salvation and sanctification of souls, or her love for the poor. Her heart burned with the "fire of divine love," which continually gave her new energy. She desired nothing except to love until she died of love.

Mother was very hardworking. Previous to her first serious heart attack in 1989, she often spent a large part of the night writing letters. Even on that last Friday, September 5, 1997, she spent the whole morning working. Her writing that day included the following general letter, which remained unsigned, as Jesus came suddenly to take her away:

Motherhouse, 5 September, 1997

My dearest children,

This brings you Mother's love, prayer and blessing that each one of you may be only all for Jesus through Mary. I know that Mother says often: "Be only all for Jesus through Mary," but that is because that is all Mother wants for you, all Mother wants for you. If in your heart you are only all for Jesus through Mary, and if you do everything only all for Jesus through Mary, you will be a true M.C.

Thank you for all the loving wishes you sent for the Society Feast. We have much to thank God for, especially that He has given us Our Lady's spirit to be the spirit of our Society. Loving Trust and Total Surrender made Our Lady say "Yes" to the message of the angel, and Cheerfulness made her run in haste to serve her cousin Elizabeth. That is so much our life—saying "Yes" to Jesus and running in haste to serve Him in the poorest of the poor. Let us keep very close to Our Lady and she will make that same spirit grow in each one of us.

September 10th is coming very close. That is another beautiful chance for us to stand near Our Lady, to listen to the thirst of Jesus and to answer with our whole heart. It is only with Our Lady that we can hear Jesus cry, "I Thirst," and it is only with Our Lady that we can thank God properly for giving this great gift to our Society. Last year was the Golden Jubilee of Inspiration Day, and I hope that the whole year has been one of thanksgiving. We will never come to the end of the gift that came to

> Mother for the Society on that day, and we must never stop thanking for it. Let our gratitude be our strong resolution to quench the thirst of Jesus by lives of real charity—love for Jesus in prayer, love for Jesus in our sisters, love for Jesus in the poorest of the poor—nothing else.
>
> And now I have heard that Jesus is giving us one more gift. This year, one hundred years after she went home to Jesus, Holy Father is declaring Little Flower to be a Doctor of the Church. Can you imagine—for doing little things with great love the Church is making her a Doctor, like St. Augustine and the big St. Teresa! It is just like Jesus said in the Gospel to the one who was seated in the lowest place, "Friend, come up higher." So let us keep very small and follow Little Flower's way of trust and love and joy, and we will fulfill Mother's promise to give saints to Mother Church.

Mother wanted to die working and to die in the room that had been hers for most of her life as a Missionary of Charity. God granted both desires.

From the moment the news of her going home to God was announced on the night of September 5, the world showed exceptional love and devotion, interest and concern. A week of vigil over her body was another form of preaching—not by mere words, nor even by action, but simply by physical presence. Thousands of people lined up to have their last "dharsan" of the little "Mahatma—Mother Teresa" and to offer their final homage to her, many bringing flowers. Throughout the world Masses and prayers were offered in thanksgiving to God for His gift of Mother Teresa to the Church and to the world.

Her funeral was unprecedented: Never before had a religious received a Catholic and state funeral at the same time. This was her final way of evangelizing the nations, when on that morning of September 13, 1997, the eyes of the whole world focused on the solemn historic event in

Calcutta. A military band accompanied the slow procession from the Church of St. Thomas, Middleton Row, to the Netaji Stadium, with Mother's corpse travelling on the funeral carriage that had been used previously for only Mahatma Gandhi and Jawaharlal Nehru, two great political leaders of the Indian nation.

Here religion and politics met in a momentary experience of heaven: the visible meeting the invisible; the Church meeting the nations. Here religions went beyond their boundaries; here political powers bowed their heads in respect and reverence to a simple religious. Here God made Himself known, once again through His humble and obedient creature Mother Teresa, as the King of Kings of the whole world. Here the words of St. Paul were manifest: "God chose what is foolish in the world to shame the wise; God chose what is weak in the world to shame the strong" (1 Cor 1:27).

Is there anything that love cannot achieve? Charity coupled with humility is the mightiest of all weapons in our struggle to conquer the world for God. Through Mother Teresa the love of God triumphed and the nations of the world bowed before the power of love—the love that can never be defeated, the love that ever conquers and goes forth to fresh victories, the love that made itself known on that solemn morning of September 13, 1997.

PART II

Letters from Mother Teresa

1971 India

A - Priest - to day - tomorrow - for ever
His chosen one.
The only one who brings
Christ on the altar
the only one who can
Say 'This is my body -
This is my blood.
and you my brother are this Priest.

God bless you 23-10-71.
Mother.

A—Priest—today—tomorrow—forever
this chosen one.
The only one who brings
Christ on the altar.
The only one who can
say: This is my body.
This is my blood.
And you my brother are this Priest.

God bless you.

Mother 23/10/71

1579 Cambria St
LDM. Los Angeles
CA-90017

Missionaries of Charity.
54A, Lower Circular Road,
Calcutta 16.

My dearest Brother Sebastian
and all at Cambria St.
If I had written all the letters
I wrote in my mind you
would have received so many.
But my prayer is each day
and everyday with each one
of you - that you may become
holy because Jesus your
God is Holy.
I am so happy you are all
well and that you are doing
God's work with great love.
Today I went to the Brothers +
gave them a long talk - Our
Vocation is to belong to Jesus
and that nothing will separate

Missionaries of Charity
54A, Lower Circular Road
Calcutta—16
For:1519 Cambria St.
Los Angeles, CA 40017

My dearest Brother Sebastian and all at Cambria St.,

If I had written all the letters I wrote in my mind you would have received so many. But my prayer is each day and everyday with each one of you—that you may become holy because Jesus your God is Holy.

I am so happy you are all well and that you are doing God's work with great love. Today I went to the Brothers and gave them a long talk. Our vocation is to belong to Jesus and that nothing will separate us from the love of Christ. How great is our vocation. How full of joy and holiness we must be out of real gratitude.

▼

us from the love of Christ
How great is our vocation.
How full of joy & holiness
we must be out of real.
gratitude.
I will be in the US. by the
17th June & I hope to be with
you at the begining of July.
then we will tell many
things to each other.
The 65 novices & 23 Sisters are
preparing for 1st & final Vows.
so you can imagen the
great fervour throughout the
house- All preparing for their
great day.
Keep the joy of Jesus as your
strength and the bond of
union & peace.

God bless you
Mother

I enclose my last letter
to the Sisters

▼

I will be in the U.S. by the 17th June and I hope to be with you at the beginning of July. Then we will tell many things to each other.

The 65 novices and 23 sisters are preparing for first and final vows, so you can imagine the great fervor throughout the house—all preparing for their great day.

Keep the joy of Jesus as your strength and the bond of union and peace.

God bless you.

Mother

I enclose my last letter to the sisters.

LDM.

Missionaries of Charity
54A, Lower Circular Road,
CALCUTTA-16,
26/10/77

Dear Brother Sebastian
Thank you for your letter of 18/10
I am praying much for you
and am more & more sure
that Jesus wants you to guide
& help the little seed of the
Brothers of the word to grow &
live – Yes, Brother I also think
the same – they need you.
You will have to get permission
from Card. Picachy – as the
Congr. of the MC Brothers is under
him – If everything is alright
with you – is it possible to
come now? the small group
needs you much. Keep in
very close contact with Sr M.
Nirmala – so that we have
One Const. Br & Srs.

Missionaries of Charity
54A, Lower Circular Road
Calcutta—16
26/10/77

Dear Brother Sebastian,

Thank you for your letter of 18/10. I am praying much for you and am more and ever sure that Jesus wants you to guide and help the little seed of the Brothers of the Word to grow and live. Yes, Brother, I also think the same—they need you.

You will have to get permission from Cardinal Picachy as the congregation of the M.C. Brothers is under him. If everything is alright with you, is it possible to come now? The small group needs you much. Keep in very close contact with Sister Nirmala so that we have one Constitution, Brother and Sister.

▼

If you can come now I would
like you to spend at least
one month in New York with
Sr M Nirmala – the Parish P.
will be very happy to have
you stay with him. We could
then work out the same Contem-
plative life of prayer & proclai-
ming of Christ – also Fr. Hardon
is there who knows my mind
very well & will help you very
much.
Dont be afraid – cling to
our Lady. I am praying much
for you to her – She will take
care of you & the Brothers you
will form for her Son.
Pray for me – by now you
must have received my letter.
God bless you
Mother

▼

If you can come now I would like you to spend at least one month in New York with Sister Nirmala. The Parish priest will be very happy to have you stay with him. We could then work out the same Constitution, some life of prayer and proclaiming of Christ. Also, Fr. Hardon is there who knows my mind very well and will help you very much.

Don't be afraid—cling to our Lady. I am praying much for you to her. She will take care of you and the Brothers you will form for her Son.

Pray for me. By now you must have received my letter.

God bless you.

Mother.
Calcutta—June, 1978

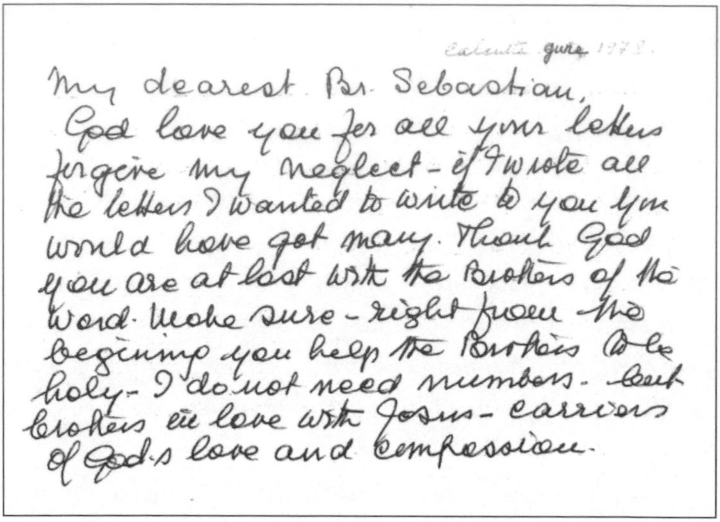

Calcutta June 1978.

My dearest Br. Sebastian,

God love you for all your letters forgive my neglect – if I wrote all the letters I wanted to write to you you would have got many. Thank God you are at last with the Brothers of the Word. Make sure – right from the beginning you help the Brothers to be holy – I do not need numbers – but brothers in love with Jesus – carriers of God's love and compassion.

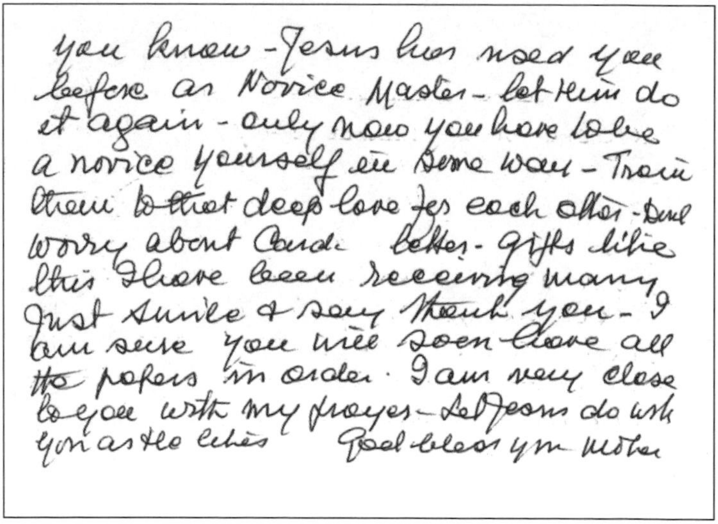

you know – Jesus has used you before as Novice Master – let Him do it again – only now you have to be a novice yourself in some way – Train them to that deep love for each other – Don't worry about cards letters – gifts like this I have been receiving many just smile & say thank you – I am sure you will soon have all the papers in order. I am very close to you with my prayers – Let Jesus do with you as He likes. God bless you Mother

Calcutta
June, 1978

My dearest Brother Sebastian,

God love you for all your letters. Forgive my neglect—if I wrote all the letters I wanted to write to you, you would have got many. Thank God you are at last with the Brothers of the Word. Make sure—right from the beginning you help the Brothers to be holy. I do not need numbers, but Brothers in love with Jesus, carriers of God's love and compassion.

You know, Jesus has used you before as Novice Master, let Him do it again, only now you have to be a novice yourself in some way. Train them to that deep love for each other. Don't worry about X's letters—gifts like this I have been receiving many. Just smile and say thank you—I am sure you will soon have all the papers in order. I am very close to you with my prayers. Let Jesus do with you as he likes.

God bless you.

Mother

+ L.D.M. December 1,1978

My dearest Children, Br. Sebastian & all in Carlo Caton

This brings you Mother's love and blessing for a very happy and Holy Christmas and God's blessing on 1979.

1978 has been so full of God's love and blessings. Our gratitude must be a resolution to make 1979 a year full of love and humility: say often during the day: "In union with all the Masses being offered throughout the world I offer Thee my Heart, make it meek and humble like yours." This year being the year of our General Chapter, let us pray more fervently, deepen our humility and increase our fidelity to our Vows, by fidelity to the small observances connected with our Vows.

Let us make sure that: Our Chastity is Chaste
Our Poverty is Total
Our Obedience is Constant
Our Charity is whole-hearted.

I ask of each one of you to remember and to put into your daily life the conviction that you are the Spouse of Jesus Crucified and that "nothing will separate you from the love of Christ" This conviction is the sure way to great Holiness - and if you are holy, you will be able to pray the work, the fruit of our holiness, that makes us contemplatives in the heart of the world.

December 1, 1978

My dearest Children, Br. Sebastian and all in Carlo Catania,

This brings your Mother's love and blessing for a very happy day and Holy Christmas and God's blessing on 1979.

1978 has been so full of God's love and blessings. Our gratitude must be a resolution to make 1979 a year full of love and humility: say often during the day: "In union with all the Masses being offered throughout the world I offer Thee my Heart, make it meek and humble like yours."

This year being the year of our General Chapter, let us pray more fervently, deepen our humility and increase our fidelity to our Vows, by fidelity to the small observances connected with our Vows.

Let us make sure that:
Our Chastity is Chaste,
Our Poverty is Total,
Our Obedience is Constant,
Our Charity is whole-hearted.

I ask of each one of you to remember and to put into your daily life the conviction that you are the Spouse of Jesus Crucified and that "nothing will separate you from the love of Christ." This conviction is the sure way to great Holiness—and if you are holy, you will be able to pray the work, the fruit of our holiness, that makes us contemplatives in the heart of the world.

▼

To be able to welcome Jesus at Christmas time not in a cold manger of our heart but in a heart full of love and humility, in a heart so pure so immaculate, so warm with love for one another.

My children, Jesus has said: "Blessed are the clean of heart for they shall see God. Let us during this month make very fervent confession and let every weekly confession be " I will go to my Father." If we imporve our daily examination of conscience immediately we will feel the need of Jesus to forgive us: we will need confession.

Let us make this resolution: Fidelity to our examination of conscience that we may be able to make a weekly fervent confession. Confession will make us pure of heart and we will see God in the appearance of bread and in the distressing disguise of the Poor.

God bless you
Mother

▼

To be able to welcome Jesus at Christmas time not in a cold manger of our heart but in a heart full of love and humility, in a heart so pure, so immaculate, so warm with love for one another.

My children, Jesus has said: "Blessed are the clean of heart for they shall see God. Let us during this month make very fervent confession and let every weekly confession be "I will go to my Father." If we improve our daily examination of conscience immediately we will feel the need of Jesus to forgive us: we will need confession.

Let us make this resolution: Fidelity to our examination of conscience that we may be able to make a weekly fervent confession. Confession will make us pure of heart and we will see God in the appearance of bread and in the distressing disguise of the Poor.

Good bless you.

Mother

Missionaries of Charity
54A, Lower Circular Road
CALCUTTA-16

LDM

New York. 16/6/79.

Dear Brother Sebastian
and all in Prenestina
The Missionaries of the W.

This brings you Mother's love and blessing. also the Good news that Br. is well and ready to be one heart full of love with you. especially with Br. Sebastian who remains the one in charge of the Pious Union. I am sure you will all be happy and willing to make any sacrifice to make your Pious Union another Nazareth - something beautiful for God -
You must have much love for each other to be able

Missionaries of Charity
54A, Lower Circular House
Calcutta—16
New York, 16/6/79

Dear Brother Sebastian and all in Prenestina, the Missionaries of the Word,

This brings you Mother's love and blessing. Also the good news that Br. X is well and ready to be one heart full of love with you. Especially with Br. Sebastian who remains the one in charge of the Pious Union. I am sure you will all be happy and willing to make any sacrifice to make your Pious Union another Nazareth, something beautiful for God.

You must have much love for each other to be able to forgive and humility to forget the past. For all is yesterday. Tomorrow has not yet come. We all have only today to love Jesus and be holy.

▼

to forgive and humility
to forget the past. For
all is Yesterday - Tomo
rrow has not yet come
we all have only to day
to love Jesus and be holy.
Be one heart my dear
Brothers - only then you
can be sure Jesus is
with you and you will
be able to give Him to
others.
Accept Br.
with love and joy as
the precious gift from
Our Lady -
Pray much for me as
I do -

God bless you
M Teresa mc

▼

Be one heart my dear Brothers—only then you can be sure Jesus is with you and you will be able to give Him to others.

Accept Br. X with love and joy, as the precious gift from Our Lady.

Pray much for me as I do .

God bless you.
Mother Teresa, M.C.

LDM. Beirut 11/8/79

My dearest children Br. Sebastian
and all in Prenistina-
This brings you Mother's love
and blessing and also
deep gratitude for the love
you gave and the joy you
shared with Mother!
God did such great things
for all of us - especially for
you - You already have
the "Mother House" before
you have the Congregation
If we only let Him do it
He does it so beautifully.
With some help I am sure
you will make it into a real
Nazareth - where Jesus can
come and rest a while
with you - I am really Happy
for you.
The difficulties that you had

Beirut, 11/8/79

My dearest children, Br. Sebastian and all the Prenistina,

This brings your Mother's love and blessing and also deep gratitude for the love you gave and the joy you shared with Mother.

God did such great things for all of us—especially for you—you already have the "Mother House" before you have the Congregation. If we only let Him do it, He does it so beautifully. With some help I am sure you will make it like a real Nazareth—where Jesus can come and rest a while with you—I am really happy for you.

The difficulties that you had were mostly due to the Carlo Catania building. The Sunshine breaks all darkness, even spiritual darkness. I saw your faces full of smiles already, thank God.

▼

were mostly due to the Carlo
Catania - Building - the
Sunshine - breaks all dar
kness - even Spiritual dar
kness - I saw your faces
full of Smiles - already
Thank God. -
I dont know if I mentioned
it to you - when the "come & see
come - please do not take them
right in - they can come
for all the prayers - but not
in the refectory & Dormitory
keep this strictly private -
Keep the joy of Poverty - only
for Jesus - keep cleanliness
with special care - Poverty
must become more & more - your
joy - Freedom - and strength.
Get Br. Gino's Brother to help you
with the garden -
I am on my way to India - may
the joy of Jesus be your love & your
strength - God bless you Mother

▼

I don't know if I mentioned it to you—when the "come and see" come please do not take them right in. They can come for all the prayers, but not in the refectory and dormitory. Keep this strictly private. Keep the joy of Poverty—only for Jesus—keep cleanliness with special care. Poverty must become more and more your joy—freedom—and strength.

Get Br. Gino's brother to help you with the garden.

I am on my way to India. May the joy of Jesus be your love and your strength.

God bless you.

Mother.

Skeu 14/8/79

My dear Brother Sebastian,
I am praying much for your family - since you told me 1st time I came to Rome and again the other day - as I told you last time - I am afraid for the little P.U. - to be left like that alone - now still less now - with Br.
Back - Please Brother make the great Sacrifice for the love of Jesus and the M.W. Same thing happened to me My Mother had not seen me for 46 years - months before she died - she kept calling, & longing to see me - her youngest child. Albania being what it is - no Indian is allowed to go - I could go so near - & yet not to her. So she died with my name in her mouth. This is why I know what

14/8/79

My dear Brother Sebastian,

I am praying much for your family since you told me first time I came to Rome and again the other day. As I told you last time, I am afraid for the little P.U., to be left like that alone, now still less now, with Br. X back. Please Brother make the great sacrifice for the love of Jesus and the Missionaries of the Word.

Same thing happened to me. My mother had not seen me for 46 years. Months before she died she kept calling and longing to see me, her youngest child. Albania being what it is, no Indian is allowed to go. I could go so near and yet not to her. So she died with my name in her mouth. This is why I know what you feel. But Our Lady will be your strength. I am asking her to take care of your family.

▼

you feel - but Our Lady will be
your strength - I am asking her
to take care of your family.
I hope Br. is at ease as
he begins his novitiate - help
him with your love and
compassion - to accept what
ever Jesus gives him
through your hands - You
know Mother's love and trust
for you and in you - so
let us together do something
beautiful for God - & for
His Glory.

Pray much for me
as I do for you.

God bless you
Mother

▼

I hope Br. X is at ease as he begins his novitiate. Help him with your love and compassion to accept whatever Jesus gives him through your hands. You know Mother's love and trust for you and in you, so let us together do something beautiful for God and for His glory.

Pray much for me, as I do for you.

God bless you.

Mother

LDM 14/8/79

My dearest Brothers,
This brings you Mother's love and blessing for the feast of the Immaculate Heart the cause of our joy and the Queen of the world. May she be more & more A Mother to each one of you for she alone is the way to Jesus She alone can give us Jesus. So let us continually turn to Her with great love.
I hope Sr. M. Nirmala was able to spend the morning with you so that more and more the same spirit and the reason for your existence be the same.
I am very sorry I left you without any greeting. The group of people you saw

Calcutta—14/8/79

My dearest Brothers,

This brings you Mother's love and blessing for the feast of the Immaculate Heart, the cause of our joy and the Queen of the World. May she be more and more a Mother to each one of you, for she alone is the way to Jesus. She alone can give us Jesus, so let us continually turn to Her with great love. I hope Sr. M. Nirmala was able to spend the morning with you, so that more and more the same spirit and the reason for your existence be the same.

I am very sorry I left you without any greeting. The group of people you saw were from Poland. The second group came for Adoration at 8 P.M. They prayed with great fervor. It was really beautiful.

My brothers, make your Community one heart full of love, another Nazareth where Jesus can come and rest a while with you. I know you will make any sacrifices, for this is the test of your love for Christ in the distressing disguise.

▼

were from Poland - the second
group came for Adoration at
8 pm. They prayed with great
fervour - It was really beau
tiful. —
My Brothers, Make your Com-
munity - one heart full
of love - another Nazareth
where Jesus can come
and rest a while with you.
I know you will make any
sacrifices - for this is the
test of your love for Christ
in the distressing disguise
My prayer as small as
it is - is very very close to
you - Help each other to grow
in holiness - Be one heart
full of love with Brother Sebastian
who even if he makes mistakes
you do not make the mistake
if you obey him - Jesus will speak
to you through him. Love & obey
him & be one heart with him - this
is all Mother asks of you. Pray for me
God bless
you Mother

▼

My prayer, as small as it is, is very, very close to you. Help each other to grow in holiness. Be one heart full of love with Brother Sebastian who, even if he makes mistakes, you do not make the mistake if you obey him. Jesus will speak to you through him. Love and obey him and be one heart with him—this is all Mother asks of you. Pray for me.

God bless.

Mother

LDM. Calcutta, 12/10/79

Dearest Brother Sebastian,

Thank you for your letter I hope you got mine. This brings you Mother's love and blessing—

1. I feel very sorry for Br. It seems that God has other plans for him—but I am really happy we gave him this last chance. I have written to Archbishop Meyer also re-him. The only thing we can do is to prey much for him—
2. I have had no news from Br. — only what you wrote. His going must have been a big sacrifice for you but if this what Jesus wants from him—it is alright.
3. Br I am sure finds it difficult—but this too—must be according to His plan.
4. I know what you feel—this

Calcutta, 12/10/79

Dearest Brother Sebastian,

Thank you for your letter. I hope you got mine. This brings you Mother's love and blessing.

1. *I feel very sorry for Br. X. It seems that God has other plans for him, but I am really happy we gave him this last chance. I have written to Archbishop Meyer also re: him. The only thing we can do is to pray much for him.*

2. *I have had no news from Br. X—only what you wrote. His going must have been a big sacrifice for you but if this is what Jesus wants from him, it is alright.*

3. *Br. X I am sure finds it difficult, but this too must be according to His plan.*

▼

really the full meaning of the Poverty of Jesus. He being rich became Poor. The riches of the company of His Father He gave up by becoming man like us in all things except sin. You too are expiriencing that "giving up" for love of him. Do not be afraid. All will be well. The seed has to die if it has to produce fruit. I am more than sure that Jesus wants the M.W. by all means to exist. & this ~~get~~ aloness is the beginning of great love. You are not alone. 'Jesus and you' Tabernacle is the most beautiful sign for you to look at when you feel lonely. Don't be afraid. He is there — inspite of the darkness & failure. It was like that for Jesus in the

▼

4. *I know what you feel—this is really the full meaning of the Poverty of Jesus. He being rich became poor. The riches of the company of His Father He gave up by becoming man like us in all things except sin. You too are experiencing that "giving up" for love of him. Do not be afraid. All will be well, the seed has to die if it has to produce fruit. I am more than sure that Jesus wants the M.W. by all means to exist. And this aloneness is the beginning of great love. You are not alone. "Jesus and you" Tabernacle is the most beautiful sign for you to look at when you feel lonely. Don't be afraid. He is there, in spite of the darkness and failure. It was like that for Jesus in the garden. "Could you not watch one hour," He felt so lonely that night. Don't be afraid. Put your hand in Our Lady's hand and walk with her.*

▼

garden - 'Could you not watch one hour' he felt so lonely that night. Don't be afraid. Put your hand in Our Lady's hand and walk with her -

Re - the house near the Vatican is that for M.W. or for the children? Let me know

I am very sure that Jesus wants to exist as M.W. among the Poorest of the Poor - even if you are only one now - it really does not matter - He has chosen you to be the one just now - dont be afraid - Jesus is with you - He will not leave you. I wish I was some where near Rome now - but dont be afraid. All this is good - because it is so like what Jesus chose for Himself.

I am sure in time vocations will come.

I enclose the letter for Br

▼

Re: the house near the Vatican is that for M.W. or for the children? Let me know.

I am very sure that Jesus wants to exist as M.W. among the Poorest of the Poor, even if you are only one now. It really does not matter. He has chosen you to be the one just now, don't be afraid. Jesus is with you. He will not leave you. I wish I was somewhere near Rome now, but don't be afraid. All this is good, because it is so like what Jesus chose for Himself. I am sure in time vocations will come.

I enclose the letter for Br. X.

▼

Have they finished with
the Constitutions - We are
trying to simplify more
ours - adding the contem
plative part - which I am
sure will help you also.
The garden must be
full of flowers - but the
flowers of your heart
must be very pleasing
to Jesus.

Keep the joy of loving
Jesus & share this
joy with all you come
in contact with

Pray much for me

God bless you

M. Teresa MC

▼

Have they finished with the Constitutions? We are trying to simplify more ours, adding the contemplative part, which I am sure will help you also. The garden must be full of flowers, but the flowers of your heart must be very pleasing to Jesus.

Keep the joy of loving Jesus and share His joy with all you come in contact with.

Pray much for me.

God bless you.

Mother Teresa, M.C.

May be you could both arrange
with Sr M Stella - Pray much for me
God bless you
Mother

Shee. 11/8/81

My dearest Brothers
Br. Sebastian and each
one of you
This brings you Mother's
love, blessing and prayer
for each one of you
that you may grow
in holiness through
Mary - the hand-
maid of the Lord - to
whom you belong in a
special way - for you
remind Her so much
of her Son Jesus.
Any news from Card Poletty
He seems to have forgotten
our existence. Please take
this letter to him and
see what he has to say

11/8/81

My dearest Brothers, Br. Sebastian and each one of you,

This brings you Mother's love, blessing and prayer for each one of you that you may grow in holiness, through Mary, the handmaid of the Lord, to whom you belong in a special way, for you remind Her so much of her Son Jesus.

Any news from Card. Poletti. He seems to have forgotten our existence. Please take this letter to him and see what he has to say.

▼

I liked your house very
much - the Chapel spe
cially - Thank God
for His gift to you -
I am on my way to Tan
zania & I hope after this
back to Calcutta - You
can imagen the letters
waiting - but it is all for
Jesus so it is alright.
Sisters from Egypt, Yemen & Eth
opia send much love and
prayer to you.
Br Sebastian I would very mu
want you to go once week - 4
houses - 4 weeks & speak on prag
& pray with them. arrange with
Sr M Stella - the day & the time
that suits you I am sure they
will profit much I have asked
Fr. Joseph also to go once week to
give an Instruction on the gospel of St Joh

▼

I liked your house very much, the Chapel especially. Thank God for His gift to you. I am on my way to Tanzania and I hope after this back to Calcutta. You can imagine the letters waiting, but it is all for Jesus so it is alright. Sisters from Egypt, Yemen and Ethiopia send much love and prayer to you.

Br. Sebastian I would very much want you to go once a week to our four houses, four weeks, and speak on prayer and pray with them. Arrange with Sr. M. Stella the day and the time that suits you. I am sure they will profit much. I have asked Fr. Joseph also to go once a week to give an instruction on the Gospel of St. John. Maybe you could both arrange with Sr. M. Stella. Pray much for me.

God bless you.

Mother

MISSIONARIES OF CHARITY
54A, Lower Circular Rd
CALCUTTA-700016

Seoul 23/11/81.

My dearest Brothers
Br. Sebastian
and all in Rome.
Thank you for all beau-
tiful letters which bring
so much good news.
Br. Andria has gone home
to God - will do and
grow into a real M.W. near
Jesus. So we have only
to ask him to pray for us
Re. Holy Father - since I am
coming we will talk it to
gether.
Thank God for the gifts of
God - so now that you

Missionaries of Charity
54A, Lower Circular Rd.
Calcutta—700016
23/11/81

My dearest Brothers, Br. Sebastian and all in Rome,

Thank you for all beautiful letters which bring so much good news. Br. Andria has gone home to God, will do and grow into a real M.W. near Jesus, so we have only to ask him to pray for us. Re: Holy Father—since I am coming we will talk it together.

Thank God for the gifts of God. So now that you are five, each one hide yourself in one of the wounds of Jesus.

▼

are five each one hide yourself
in one of the wounds of Jesus.
I am very happy & thank God
for the light God had given
you re- the priest. Brother.
I am happy to know Br. Piet
is at Beda's. Please let us
pray together & then speak
about it - to Card. Poletti &
others for God will speak
in the silence of the
heart & we can speak
then from the fulness
of our hearts
In 2 weeks time I will
be with you please God
in the mean time let
us pray.

God bless you
M. Teresa MC

▼

I am very happy and thank God for the light God has given you, re: the priest Brother.

I am happy to know Br. Piet is at Beda. Please let us pray together and then speak about it to Card. Poletti and others, for God will speak in the silence of the heart and we can speak then from the fullness of our hearts.

In two weeks time I will be with you please God. In the meantime let us pray.

God bless you.

Mother Teresa, M.C.

SDM. 20/1/82

My dear Br. Sebastian.

Thank you for your lett.
I am so glad to hear that
you all had such a beautiful
Christmas - Yes M.W. keeps
growing from within - this
more important than
anything in the world.
I hope by now Br. i
with you
Re - your people at home - may
be you should come now - as
once the regular Nov. begin
you will not be able to move.
try to get one of cheap flights
return ticket -
I hope all the Brothers are
well - and are growing

20/1/82

My dear Br. Sebastian,

Thank you for your letter. I am so glad to hear that you all had such a beautiful Christmas. Yes, M.W. keeps growing from within, this more important than anything in the world.

I hope by now Br. X is with you. Re—your people at home—maybe you should come now, as once the regular Novitiate begins you will not be able to move. Try to get one of cheap flights return ticket.

▼

in holiness through
love for each other God
will take care of Number
in His own good time
Help the brothers more
and more to unders
tand – it is not how
much we do for God
but how much love
we put in the doing
Keep the joy of loving
Jesus in your heart
and share this joy
with all you meet
especially your brothers
Let us pray

God bless you
Mother

▼

I hope all the Brothers are well and are growing in holiness through love for each other. God will take care of numbers in His own good time. Help the Brothers more and more to understand—it is not how much we do for God but how much love we put in the doing. Keep the joy of loving Jesus in your heart and share this joy with all you meet, especially your Brothers.

Let us pray.

God bless you.

Mother

1.

MISSIONARIES OF CHARITY
54A ACHARYA J. CHANDRA BOSE
CALCUTTA 700016, INDIA

LDM.

1990

My dearest children, Sisters Brothers, Fathers, Lay Missionaries Co-workers.

This brings you my prayer and blessing for each one of you - my love and gratitude to each one of you for all you have been and have done all these 40 years to share the joy of loving each other and the Poorest of the Poor.

Your presence and the work you have done throughout the world for the glory of God and the good of the Poor has been a living miracle of love of God and yours in action God has shown His greatness by

Missionaries of Charity
54A Acharya J. Chandra Bose
Calcutta, 700016, India

My dearest children, Sisters, Brothers, Fathers, Lay Missionaries, Co-workers,

This brings you my prayer and blessing for each one of you, my love and gratitude to each one of you for all you have been and have done all these 40 years to share the joy of loving each other and the Poorest of the Poor.

Your presence and the work you have done throughout the world for the glory of God and the good of the Poor has been a living miracle of love of God and yours in action. God has shown His greatness by using nothingness, so let us always remain in our nothingness, so as to give God free hand to use us without consulting us.

▼

using nothingness - so let us always remain in our nothingness - so as to give God free hand to use us without consulting us.

Let us accept whatever He gives and give whatever He takes with a big smile.

As the days of the General Chapter draw near my heart is filled with joy and expectation - of the beautiful things God will do through each one of you by accepting with joy the One God has chosen to be our Superior General. Beautiful are the ways of God if we allow Him to use us as He wants.

▼

Let us accept whatever He gives and give whatever He takes with a big smile.

As the days of the General Chapter draw near my heart is filled with joy and expectation of the beautiful things God will do through each one of you by accepting with joy the One God has chosen to be our Superior General. Beautiful are the ways of God if we allow Him to use us as He wants.

▼

MISSIONARIES OF CHARITY
54A ACHARYA J. CHANDRA BOSE
CALCUTTA 700016, INDIA

I am still in Eastern Europe
The living Miracles God has
done during these days have
been a prof of His tender
love for His MC. and our Poor.
Let our gratitude be our
strong resolution to be
only all for Jesus through
Mary. Let us be Pure and
Humble like Mary and we
are sure to be Holy like
Jesus.
Humility always is the root
of zeal for souls and Charity
We see that in Jesus - on the
cross and in the Eucharist
We see it in Mary - went in haste
to serve as hand Maid - not as
Mother of God.

▼

I am still in Eastern Europe. The living Miracles God has done during these days have been a proof of His tender love for this M.C. and our Poor.

Let our gratitude be our strong resolution to be only all for Jesus through Mary. Let us be Pure and Humble like Mary and we are sure to be Holy like Jesus.

Humility always is the root of zeal for our souls and charity. We see that in Jesus on the cross and in the Eucharist. We see it in Mary, went in haste to serve as handmaid, not as Mother of God.

▼

so it is very important for us
MC. to be pure and humble
No MC. can live a true MC.
life and the 4th vow without
a pure and humble heart.
because a pure heart can
see God in the Poor - a humble
heart can love and serve
Jesus in the Poor.
Remember the five fingers
You - did - it - to - Me
Remember - Love begins at
home - our Community - our
family.
Remember - Works of love are
works of Peace.
Let us thank Jesus for the 40
years of tender love we have
received from Him through
each other - and pray that we

▼

So it is very important for us M.C. to be pure and humble. No M.C. can live a true M.C. life and the 4th vow without a pure and humble heart, because a pure heart can see God in the Poor, a humble heart can love and serve Jesus in the Poor.

Remember the five fingers: You-did-it-to-Me.

Remember, love begins at home, our community, our family.

Remember, works of love are works of Peace.

Let us thank Jesus for the 40 years of tender love we have received from Him through each other, and pray that we grow in this love for each other and our Poor, by deepening our personal and intimate love for Jesus and greater attachment to Jesus through Prayer and Sacrifice.

▼

MISSIONARIES OF CHARITY
54A ACHARYA J. CHANDRA BOSE
CALCUTTA 700016, INDIA

grow in this love for each other and our Poor – by deepening our personal and intimate love for Jes and greater attachment to Jesus through Prayer and Sacrifice.
Try to be Jesus' love, Jesus' compassion – Jesus' presenc to each other and the Poor you serve.
All this will be possible if you keep close to Mary the Mother of Jesus and our Mother. She will guide & protec you and keep you only all for Jesus.
Let nothing and nobody ever separate you from the love

▼

Try to be Jesus' love, Jesus' compassion, Jesus' presence to each other and the Poor you serve.

All this will be possible if you keep close to Mary the Mother of Jesus and our Mother. She will guide and protect you and keep you only all for Jesus.

Let nothing and nobody ever separate you from the love of Jesus and Mary. It was at Her pleading that the Society was born. Let it again be at Her pleading that the Society gives Saints to Mother Church.

▼

of Jesus and Mary—It was at Her pleading that the Society was born—let it be again at Her pleading that the Society gives Saints to Mother Church.

Remember wherever you may be—Mother's prayer love and blessing will always be with you

God bless you
M. Teresa MC

▼

Remember wherever you may be, Mother's prayer, love and blessing will always be with you.

God bless you.

Mother Teresa, M.C.

MISSIONARIES OF CHARITY

"As long as you did it to one of these My least brethren, You did it to Me"

Rome. 16/6/93

LDM.

Our Dear Holy Father,

It was a real gift of God to be present at the Holy Mass with You to pray with You and receive Jesus from You.

To day I come together with Fr. Sebastian my Co-founder, with good news to offer You a gift.

As you know Missionaries of Charity keep growing with God's blessing. We now have Sisters active and contemplative, Brothers and Priests.

Since March 19th 1979 we have a Pious Union known as Missionaries of Charity Brothers Contemplative in the Diocese of Rome. After much prayer and and sacrifice I feel this is the time for the Brothers to become a diocesen Religious Institute. For this I appeal to You to help us that the Church will grant us this gift.

At present they are 24 Brothers working in Rome, Albania and Brazil.

The very beautiful gift of God has given to the Brothers is to begin the Lay Missionaries of Charity movement for the families. They have already 500 families through out the world who have Consecrated their

Rome, 16/6/93

Our Dear Holy Father,

It was a real gift of God to be present at the Holy Mass with you, to pray with you and receive Jesus from you.

Today I come together with Fr. Sebastian, my co-founder, with good news to offer you a gift.

As you know Missionaries of Charity keep growing with God's blessing. We now have Sisters active and contemplative, Brothers and Priests.

Since March 19th 1979 we have a Pious Union known as Missionaries of Charity Brothers Contemplative in the Diocese of Rome. After much prayer and sacrifice I feel this is the time for the Brothers to become a diocesan Religious Institute. For this I appeal to you to help us that the Church will grant us this gift.

At present they are 24 Brothers working in Rome, Albania and Brazil.

The very beautiful gift that God has given to the Brothers is to begin the Lay Missionaries of Charity movement for the families. They have already 500 families throughout the world who have consecrated their lives to live their lives through prayer and the vows of Poverty, Chastity, Obedience and whole-hearted free service to the Poorest of the Poor, as per their married life permits. This Consecration has been a very great gift of God to the families, so please Holy Father pray for them and bless them.

▼

MISSIONARIES OF CHARITY

"As long as you did it to one of these My least brethren, You did it to Me"

lives to live their lives through prayer and the Vows of Poverty, Chastity, Obedience and whole Hearted free service to the Poorest of the Poor, as per their married life permits – This Consecration has been a very great gift of God to the families. so please Holy Father pray for them and bless them.

Father and I come to You with our whole heart and profund humility, with the help of Mary our Mother to help us become a diocesan Religious Institute, since this branch is still only a Pious Union.

Please Holy Father bless your devoted Missionaries of Charity that they become true Contemplatives, fully Consecrated to God and His Church – so that whatever they do be done for the glory of God and the good of the Church.

Please Holy Father pray for Fr. Sebastian and for me Your devoted children in Mary

Fr. Sebastian m c — Registered Charity C No 37184 C.T. 8E/1454-55 — M. Teresa mc

▼

Father and I come to you with our whole heart and profound humility, with the help of Mary our Mother to help us become a diocesan Religious Institute, since this branch is still only a Pious Union.

Please Holy Father bless your devoted Missionaries of Charity that they become true Contemplatives, fully consecrated to God and His Church so that whatever they do be done for the glory of God and the good of the Church.

Please Holy Father pray for Fr. Sebastian and for me—Your devoted children in Mary.

Father Sebastian, M.C.

Mother Teresa, M.C.

LM My dear Lay Missionaries

Keep the joy of loving Jesus in your heart and share this joy with all you meet

Make a strong resolution " I will, I want, with God's blessing be holy"

This will help you to satiate the Thirst of Jesus for love for souls – by working at the Salvation and the Sanctification of the Poorest of the Poor – specially your family.

Let us pray

God bless you
M Teresa MC

Rome 9-12-93

Rome 9/12/93

My dear Lay Missionaries,

Keep the joy of loving Jesus in your heart and share this joy with all you meet. Make a strong resolution "I will, I want, with God's blessing be holy."

This will help you to satiate the thirst of Jesus for love for souls, by working at the Salvation and the Sanctification of the Poorest of the Poor, especially your family.

Let us pray.

God bless you,
Mother Teresa, M.C.

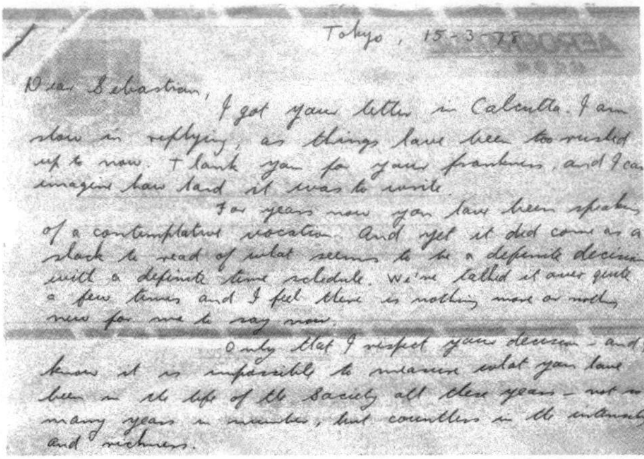

Tokyo, 15-3-78

Dear Sebastian,

I got your letter in Calcutta. I am slow in replying, as things have been too rushed up to now. Thank you for your frankness, and I can imagine how hard it was to write.

For years now you have been speaking of a contemplative vocation. And yet it did come as a shock to read of what seems to be a definite decision with a definite time schedule. We've talked it over quite a few times and I feel there is nothing more or nothing new for me to say now.

Only that I respect your decision – and I know it is impossible to measure what you have been in the life of the Society all these years – not so many years in number, but countless in the intensity and richness.

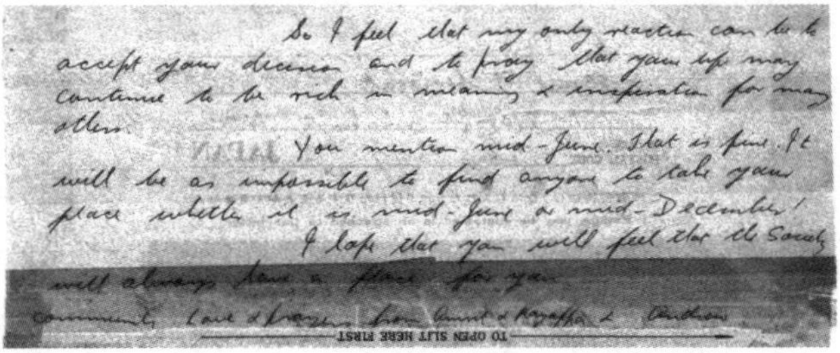

So I feel that my only reaction can be to accept your decision and to pray that your life may continue to be rich in meaning & inspiration for many others.

You mention mid-June. That is fine. It will be as impossible to find anyone to take your place whether it is mid-June or mid-December!

I hope that you will feel that the Society will always have a place for you.

community. Love & prayers from Anand & Kayappa & Anthony

TO OPEN SLIT HERE FIRST

Tokyo, 15/3/78

Dear Sebastian,

I got your letter in Calcutta. I am slow in replying, as things have been too rushed up to now. Thank you for your frankness, and I can imagine how hard it was to write.

For years now you have been speaking of a contemplative vocation. And yet it did come as a shock to read of what seems to be a definite decision with a definite time schedule. We've talked it over quite a few times and I feel there is nothing more or nothing new for me to say now.

Only that I respect your decision, and know it is impossible to measure what you have been in the life of the Society all these years—not many years in number, but countless in the intensity and richness.

So I feel that my only reaction can be to accept your decision and to pray that your life may continue to be rich in meaning and inspiration for many others.

You mention mid-June. That is fine. It will be as impossible to find anyone to take your place whether it is mid-June or mid-December.

I hope that you will find that the Society will always have a place for you.

With affection and prayers,

Brother Andrew

PART III

Photos

Rome, March 1989. Fr. Sebastian and Mother Teresa on her visit to the contemplative brothers' house on Via di S. Agapito.

October 7, 1950. Mother Teresa (third on the left up) and the first group of the Missionary Sisters of Charity on the day they started the novitiate.

Fr. Sebastian (left) and Fr. Joseph Neuner, S.J., spiritual father to Mother Teresa and to Fr. Sebastian and theology professor in Pune in the seventies.

October 24, 1971, Fr. Sebastian's first Holy Mass. Fr. Sebastian (left) and Fr. Leo Donnelly, S.J., his spiritual father and philosophy professor in Ranchi.

Calcutta, 1975. Fr. Sebastian (middle) in front of the Missionaries of Charity Brothers' house at 7, Mansatala Row.

Brother Andrew, co-founder of the Missionaries of Charity Brothers.

Calcutta, June 1975. Brother Andrew and Fr. Sebastian.

Los Angeles, 1977. Fr. Sebastian speaks at the Hilton Hotel about poverty and in particular about the poor in Los Angeles.

Los Angeles, July 1977. Mother Teresa's visit to the Missionaries of Charity Brothers' house.

Los Angeles, July 1977. Fr. Sebastian and Patty Kump, at that time responsible for the coworkers of Mother Teresa in the United States.

Los Angeles, July 5, 1977. Fr. Sebastian (left) awaits Mother Teresa's departure from Los Angeles airport after her three-day visit with the Missionaries of Charity Brothers.

New York, April 28, 1978. Fr. Sebastian and Mother Teresa in the garden behind the Missionaries of Charity Sisters' house in the Bronx.

Rome, December 13, 1979. Mother Teresa with her brother Lazar (left) visit the house of the Missionaries of Charity Brothers Contemplative on Via di S. Agapito.

Rome, December 13, 1979. Mother Teresa and Fr. Sebastian with the Holy Father after she received the Nobel Peace Prize.

Rome, December 13, 1979. Mother Teresa and the Holy Father with the Missionaries of Charity Sisters and Fr. Sebastian on a visit to the Vatican

Zagreb, 1981. Fr. Sebastian (second from left) with some Missionaries of Charity Sisters.

Rome, July 11, 1984. Maria Pia Fanfani reads during the Holy Mass presided over by his Eminence Ugo Cardinal Poletti at the blessing of the restored home of the Missionaries of Charity Brothers Contemplative.

Rome, November 7, 1984. (From left) Br. Piet, Cardinal U. Poletti, and Fr. Sebastian.

Rome, November 7, 1984. Fr. Sebastian (center) and Cardinal U. Poletti on the occasion of the blessing of the contemplative brothers' residence.

Rome, April 16, 1984. The first group of the Lay Missionaries of Charity and Mother Teresa on the day of their first profession in the chapel of the Missionaries of Charity Brothers Contemplative on Via di S. Agapito.

Father Ivan Marie in prayer.

Rome, May 26, 1985, Pentecost Sunday. Mother Teresa and Fr. Sebastian at the Holy Mass in thanksgiving for the new names "Missionaries of Charity—Contemplative" and "Lay Missionaries of Charity."

Rome, May 26, 1985. Mother Teresa's talk during the Holy Mass of thanksgiving.

Rome, May 26, 1985. Mother Teresa receives Holy Communion from Fr. Sebastian's hands.

Calcutta, February 1986. The Holy Father and Mother Teresa in the home for the dying during his apostolic visit in India.

Rome. The Holy Father and Mother Teresa.

Rome, March 1989. Fr. Sebastian and Mother Teresa on her visit to the contemplative brothers' house on Via di S. Agapito.

Rome, 1989. The Holy Father signs the plans for *Casa Serena,* the night shelter on Via di S. Agapito for the poorest of the poor.

Rome, May 2, 1990. Fr. Sebastian and Mother Teresa in the Missionaries of Charity Sisters' house in S. Gregorio al Celio.

Calcutta, September 27, 1990. Mother Teresa and Fr. Sebastian during the extraordinary general chapter of the Missionaries of Charity Sisters.

Rome, May 26, 1991. Mother Teresa during the first Holy Mass of Br. André Marie at the house of the Missionaries of Charity Brothers Contemplative.

Rome, May 26, 1991. First Holy Mass of Br. André Marie. Fr. Sebastian (center), Mother Teresa, and Sr. Agnes, who was the first to join Mother as a Missionaries of Charity Sisters.

Rome, May 29, 1993. Mother Teresa with Fr. Sebastian and Br. Damien on the occasion of the jubilee of their religious profession.

Rome, May 29, 1993. (From left) Fr. Sebastian, Archbishop Giuseppe Mani, and Br. Damien on the jubilee of the brothers' religious professions and the blessing of *Casa Serena,* the night shelter for men run by the contemplative brothers with the help of the Lay Missionaries of Charity and volunteers.

Rome, June 16, 1993. Mother Teresa reads the Holy Father the letter in which she asks for diocesan recognition of the Missionaries of Charity Brothers Contemplative.

Bushat, August 18, 1993. Mother Teresa during Holy Mass with the contemplative brothers during her visit to Albania.

Bushat, Shkodra, August 18, 1993. A ray of sunlight on Mother Teresa's face at Holy Mass during her visit to the brothers' house in Albania.

Bushat, August 18, 1993. The church and the house of the Missionaries of Charity Brothers Contemplative in Albania.

Rome, December 31, 1993. Final vows of the first group of the contemplative brothers after the recognition of the congregation as a diocesan institute. Archbishop Giuseppe Mani presided at the Holy Mass.

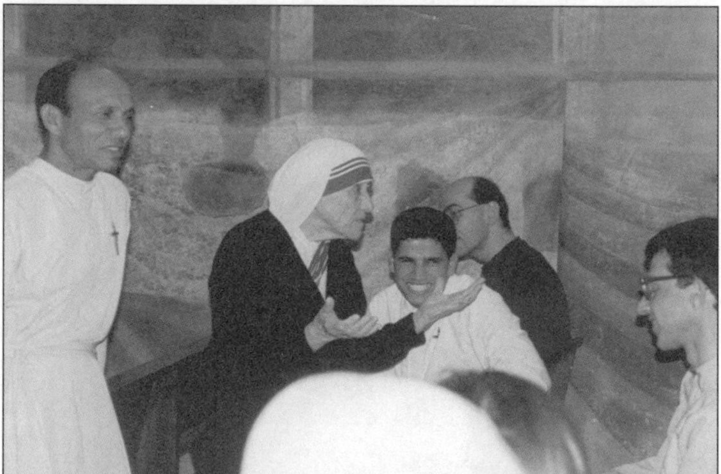

Rome, 1994. (From left) Br. Charbel, Mother Teresa, and Fr. Sebastian in *Dono di Maria,* "the Gift of Mary," the sisters' house in the Vatican.

Gurgaon, India, November 18, 1995. (From left) Br. André Marie, Br. Damien, Mother Teresa, and Fr. Sebastian on the inauguration and blessing of *Deepashram*, "House of Light," the contemplative brothers' house for orphaned handicapped boys.

Calcutta, September 8, 1996. First profession of some of the contemplative brothers in the motherhouse of the Missionaries of Charity Sisters.

Calcutta, September 8, 1996. Some Sisters dancing for the newly professed brothers.

Calcutta, September 8, 1996. Group photo of Missionaries of Charity Sisters and the newly professed contemplative brothers in the motherhouse.

Lourdes, September 1996. Second international meeting of the Lay Missionaries of Charity.

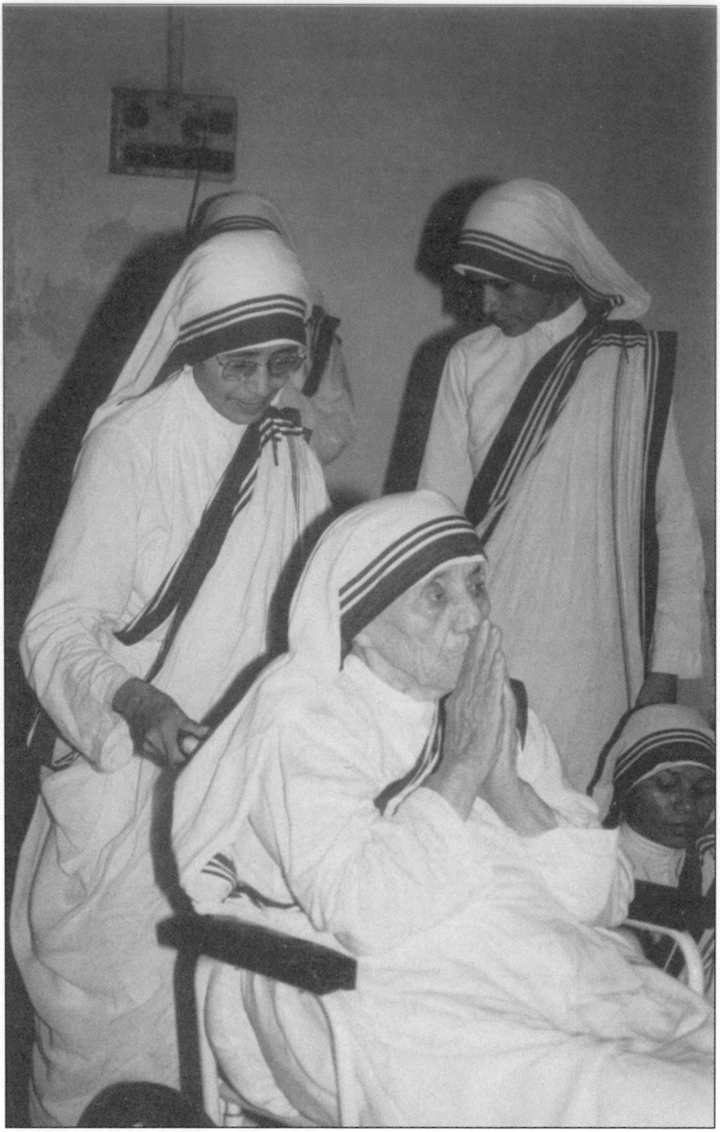

Rome, May 1997. Sr. Nirmala, the present superior general of the Missionary Sisters of Charity, with Mother Teresa.

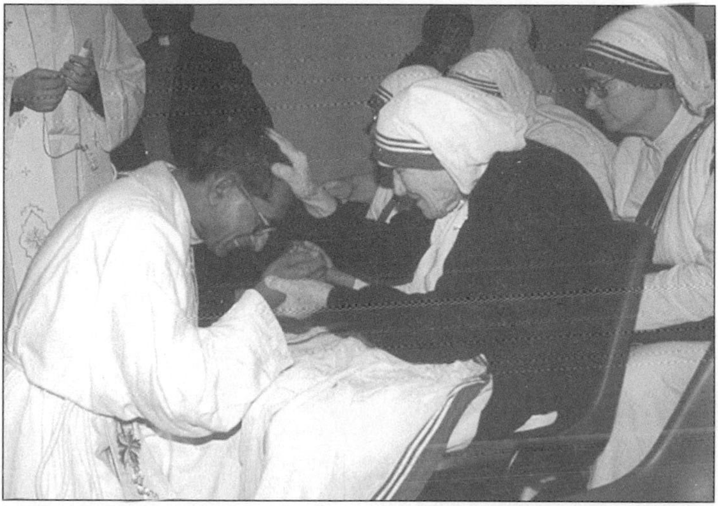

Rome, May 1997. Mother Teresa and Br. Damien in the Missionaries of Charity Sisters' house on Via Casilina.

Rome, May 1997. Mother Teresa and Fr. Sebastian in the Missionaries of Charity Sisters' house on Via Casilina.

Rome, May 20, 1997. Fr. Sebastian (left) and Mother Teresa visit the Holy Father.

Rome, July 19, 1997. Mother Teresa meets the contemplative brothers on Via Casilina for the last time and gives a long talk on humility.

Rome, July 19, 1997. Mother Teresa and Fr. Sebastian with a group of people after Holy Mass.

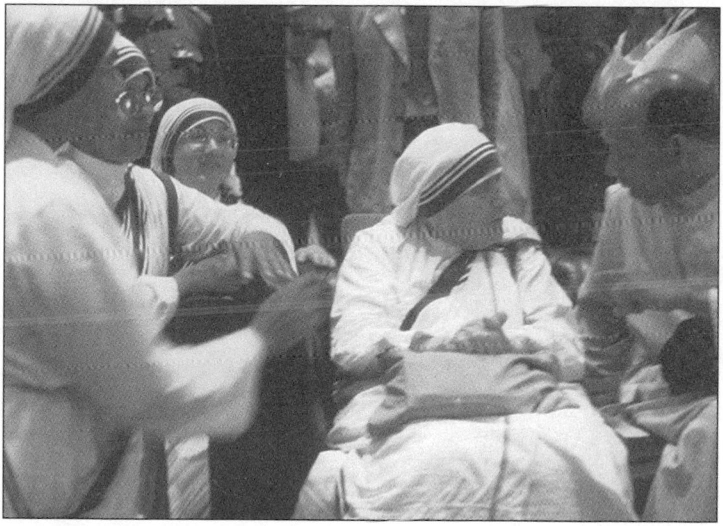

Rome, July 19, 1997. Fr. Sebastian and Mother Teresa wait for the airplane that will take Mother back to Calcutta for the last time.

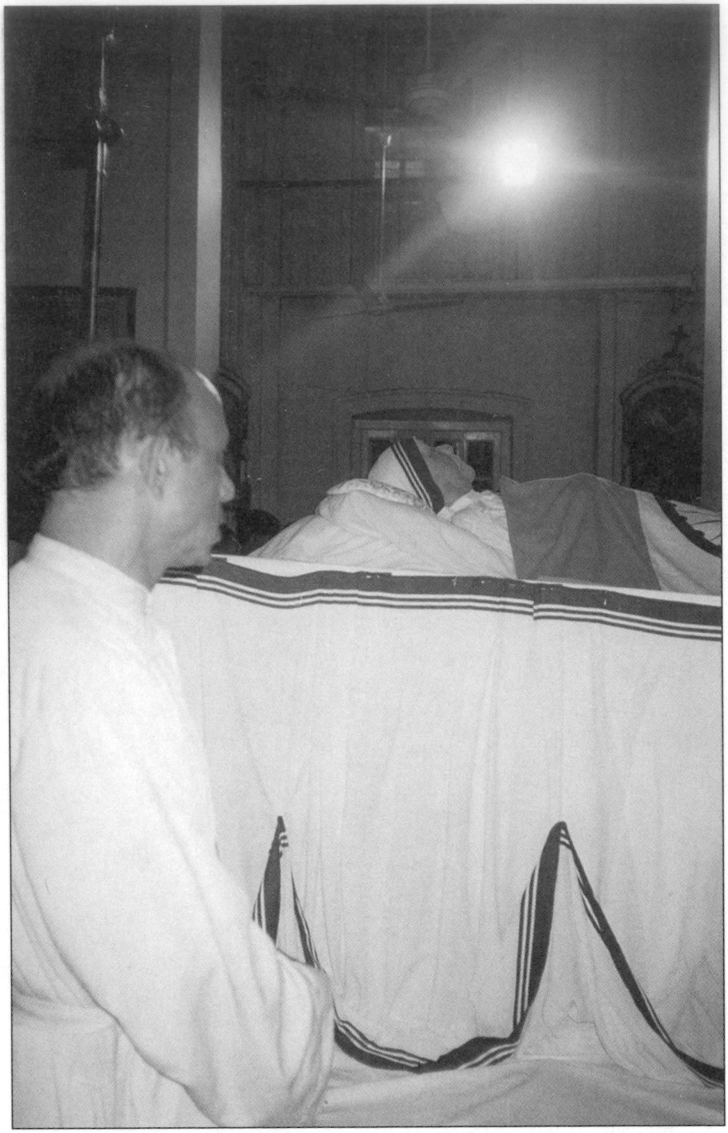

Calcutta, September 1997. Fr. Sebastian keeps vigil
beside Mother's body.

Rome, September 5, 2000. Fr. Sebastian and the Holy Father on the third anniversary of Mother Teresa's death.

Rome, September 5, 2000. Fr. Sebastian and the Holy Father on the third anniversary of Mother Teresa's death.

Rome, St. John Lateran. Fr. Sebastian (center) and the Lay Missionaries of Charity, gathered in preparation for their general chapter.

Assisi, July 13, 2002. The third international meeting and first general chapter of the Lay Missionaries of Charity, founded by Fr. Sebastian with the approval of Mother Teresa on April 16, 1984.

PART IV

The Guiding Principles of the Missionaries of Charity Brothers Contemplative

The Guiding Principles of the Missionaries of Charity Brothers Contemplative

The spiritual dynamic that characterizes our branch is expressed in terms of prayer, penance, and works of mercy, the three "acts of religion," according to the *Catechism of the Catholic Church*. Jesus, our Divine Master, wants the Missionaries of Charity Brothers Contemplative to love and serve Him in the distressing disguise of the poorest of the poor in joyful praise, thanksgiving, intercession, and reparation (our Constitutions, Rule 100). This is done mainly through prayer, penance, and works of mercy, both spiritual and corporal; thus we strive to satiate the infinite thirst of Jesus on the cross for love of souls.

Since it is never the will of our Father in heaven that one of these little ones should be lost (see Mt 18:14), Jesus wants us to go in search of the lost sheep, calling them to repentance. He wants us to instruct the ignorant while counseling the doubtful. There are so many sorrow-filled people to be comforted. Amazingly enough, to bear wrongs patiently and to forgive injuries are spiritual works of mercy, as is praying for the living and the dead.

In the evening of life, when we appear before God, we will be judged according to the works of mercy:

> "Come, you that are blessed by my Father, inherit the kingdom prepared for you from the foundation of the world; for I was hungry and you gave me food, I was thirsty and you gave me something to drink, I was a stranger and you welcomed me, I was naked and you gave me clothing, I was sick and you took care of me, I was in prison and you visited me." Then the righteous will answer him, "Lord, when was it that we saw you hungry... thirsty... a stranger... or naked...?" And the

> king will answer them, "Truly I tell you, just as you did it to one of the least of these who are members of my family, you did it to me."—MATTHEW 25:34-38, 40

Whenever, therefore, we feed the hungry, clothe the naked, shelter the homeless, take care of the sick, visit the prisoners, we do it to Jesus. The Jesus whom we contemplate, love, and adore in the Bread of Life—with respect, faith, and devotion—is the same Jesus whom we are called to meet, love, and serve with the self-same respect, faith, and devotion in the distressing disguise of the poorest of the poor. "How could it be otherwise, since the Christ encountered in contemplation is the same who lives and suffers in the poor?" (John Paul II, *Vita Consecrata,* "Apostolic Exhortation on the Consecrated Life and Its Mission in the Church and in the World," March 25, 1996, 82). Our Constitutions also says: "From the presence of Jesus in the Blessed Sacrament we go to the presence of Jesus in the poorest of the poor and vice versa" (Rule 5).

Our God then is neither a silent spectator nor a disinterested listener; He knows everything about us. He takes into consideration all that we do.

> God is not unjust; he will not overlook your work and the love that you showed for his sake in serving the saints, as you still do. And we want each one of you to show the same diligence so as to realize the full assurance of hope to the very end, so that you may not become sluggish, but imitators of those who through faith and patience inherit the promises.—HEBREWS 6:10-12

Jesus was a man of prayer and of great penance and sacrifice. He prayed and fasted for forty days in the desert: "He ate nothing at all during those days" (Lk 4:2); "He went out to the mountain to pray; and he spent the night in prayer to God" (Lk 6:12); "In the morning, while it was still very dark, he got up and went out to a deserted place, and there he prayed" (Mk 1:35). Before performing any miracles Jesus prayed to the Father: "Jesus looked upward and said, 'Father, I thank you for having heard me. I knew that you always hear me'" (Jn 11:41-42); "Jesus took with him Peter and John and James, and went up on the mountain to pray" (Lk 9:28).

Jesus not only prayed before His passion but also asked His apostles to stay awake with Him: "He threw himself on the ground and prayed.... 'Simon are you asleep? Could you not keep awake one hour?'" (Mk 14:35, 37). Jesus also prayed for His enemies before giving up His life on the Cross: "Father, forgive them; for they do not know what they are doing" (Lk 23:34). His death on the cross was a great act of prayer: "'Father, into your hands I commend my spirit.' Having said this, he breathed his last" (Lk 23:46).

Jesus' whole life was a continuous prayer, filled with sacrifice and penance. Long fasts, vigils for entire nights, filled with cries and tears: "In the days of his flesh, Jesus offered up prayers and supplications, with loud cries and tears.... Although he was a Son, he learned obedience through what he suffered; and having been made perfect, he became the source of eternal salvation for all who obey him" (Heb 5: 7, 8-9).

Jesus has not only set a remarkable example of prayer and sacrifice but invites all His followers to take up their crosses every day: "If any want to become my followers, let them deny themselves and take up their cross daily and follow me" (Lk 9:23). He also wants us to pray continually—day and night—and never lose heart. "Will not God grant justice to his chosen ones who cry to him day and night?" (Lk 18:7).

We also see the apostles follow the example of the

Master. Soon after the ascension of Jesus, the apostles "were constantly devoting themselves to prayer, together with certain women, including Mary, the Mother of Jesus, as well as his brothers" (Acts 1:14).

Jesus not only left the Church a great patrimony of prayer and penance but, even more, He also gave us a rich heritage of works of mercy: "He had compassion for them and cured their sick" (Mt 14:14); "Jesus called his disciples to him and said, 'I have compassion for the crowd because they have been with me now for three days and have nothing to eat; and I do not want to send them away hungry, for they might faint on the way'" (Mt 15:32). When Jesus saw the widow of Nain, "he had compassion for her and said to her, 'Do not weep.' Then he came forward and touched the bier" (Lk 7:13-14); "Jesus, tired out by his journey, was sitting by the well" and asked the Samaritan woman for a drink (see Jn 4:6-29). We can easily say that Jesus' life on earth was an uninterrupted work of prayer, penance, and mercy.

Our holy, Catholic, and apostolic Church, then, is built on prayer, penance, and works of mercy: All of them contribute to her basic structure. If prayer is the life-breath of the Church, sacrifice and penance are the skeleton, and works of mercy the flesh. Therefore there must be a harmonious balance among these basic elements.

In the first place, Jesus wants us to be men of prayer, and this is also the mind of the Church, as we read in Canon 663, paragraph 1: "Contemplation of divine things and assiduous union with God in prayer is to be the first and foremost duty of all religious." He also wants us to share the overflow of our experience of God with others, especially with the poor: "Give, and it will be given to you. A good measure, pressed down, shaken together, running over, will be put into your lap; for the measure you give will be the measure you get back" (Lk 6:38). We are called to proclaim "what we have heard, what we have seen with our eyes, what we have looked at and touched with our hands" (1 Jn 1:1).

At times people ask us, "Aren't you contemplatives? Then how can you have homes for homeless people of the street or for homeless handicapped boys, and so on?" These questions and comments are quite legitimate and appropriate, as we are the contemplative expression of the Missionaries of Charity founded by Mother Teresa of Calcutta. We too like St. Benedict have a program of *ora et labora*. But our *labora* time is spent with the poor.

> The Gospel is made effective through charity, which is the Church's glory and the sign of her faithfulness to the Lord. This is demonstrated by the whole history of the consecrated life, which can be considered a living exegesis of Jesus' words: "As you did it to the one of the last of these my brethren, you did it to me" (Mt 25:40). Many institutes, especially in modern times, were established precisely to address one or other of the needs of the poor. But even when such a purpose was not the determining factor, concern and care for the needy—expressed in prayer, assistance and hospitality—was always a normal part of every form of the consecrated life, even of the contemplative life. And how could it be otherwise, since the Christ encountered in contemplation is the same who lives and suffers in the poor? In this sense, the history of the consecrated life is rich with marvellous and sometimes ingenious examples. Saint Paulinus of Nola, after distributing his belongings to the poor in order to consecrate his life fully to God, built the cells of his monastery above a hospice for the poor. He rejoiced at the thought of this singular "exchange of gifts": the poor, whom he helped, strengthened with

> their prayers the very "foundations" of his house, wholly dedicated to the praise of God. Saint Vincent de Paul, for his part, loved to say that, when one is obliged to leave prayer to attend to a poor person in need, that prayer is not really interrupted, because "one leaves God to serve God." (Vita Consecrata 82)

"You have such a beautiful opportunity to take care of Jesus in the poor and be real contemplatives" (Mother Teresa).

The word *contemplative,* then, need not only be explained and understood in a purely traditional sense, but it can also be explained, understood, and lived in a different way. There can be new approaches to the whole concept of contemplation, and a new way of living one's contemplative vocation. We can also be walking contemplatives, contemplatives on the road. As prayer is a necessary means for continual contact with God, so any and every authentic love-filled activity of man can also be a means of union with God.

There can be pure mental contemplation and there can also be active contemplation; even more, there can be real contemplation in action. A genuine contemplative is also a true missionary. This can be seen in the example of St. Thérèse of Lisieux, who has been proclaimed the patroness of the missions together with St. Francis Xavier. The former was a contemplative missionary, while the latter was a missionary contemplative. The modality or the way and manner of contemplating can be different, but the essential elements are the same.

Contemplatives must not only know the techniques of contemplation but must have the ability to use any material for contemplation, even so-called "profane" or "worldly" realities. In this context we can learn again from St. Thérèse, who writes: "I accept all distractions for the love of God, even the wildest fancies that cross my mind." This is the acid test of a true contemplative. With humility and serene confidence a contemplative brother tries to transform the profane into sacred. He not only purifies it but then even perfumes it with the virtues of faith, hope, and charity. The result is a profound and deepening sense of peace and joy, which is part of an ongoing process that ends with the beatific vision.

Jesus wants us to bear witness in every situation that we belong to Him. The religious habit that we wear is a sign of consecration, poverty, and membership (see *Vita Consecrata,* 25). We are Jesus' soldiers who have been called to fight constantly against our spiritual enemies: the world, the devil, and the flesh. It is the work of soldiers to protect and safeguard their country even with their lives. How much more then must we religious remain loyal to Jesus, the King of Kings and the Lord of Lords, even to the point of shedding our blood!

In conclusion we can say, together with St. Peter Chrysologus:

> There are three things by which faith stands firm, devotion remains constant, and virtue endures. They are prayer, penance and works of mercy. Prayer knocks at the door, penance obtains and works of mercy receive... These three are one and they give light to each other.
>
> Penance is the soul of prayer, works of mercy are the life-blood of penance. Let no one try to separate them... If you pray, fast; if you fast, show mercy; if you want your petition to be heard, hear the petition of others. If you do not close your ear to others, you open God's ear to yourself.
>
> When you fast, see the fasting of others. If you want God to know that you are hungry, know that another is hungry. If you hope for mercy, show mercy. If you look

for kindness, show kindness. If you want to receive, give. If you ask for yourself what you deny to others, your asking is a mockery....

Let prayer, penance and works of mercy be one single plea to God on our behalf, one speech in our defence, a threefold united prayer in our favour. (See St. Peter Chrysologus' Sermon 43, Office of Readings for Tuesday, Lent, week 3.)